Academic Writing, Philosophy and Genre

Academic Writing, Philosophy and Genre

Edited by
Michael A. Peters

WILEY-BLACKWELL

A John Wiley & Sons, Ltd., Publication

This edition first published 2009
Originally published as Volume 40, Issue 7 of *Educational Philosophy and Theory*, except for chapter 7 ('Philosophy as Literature' by Jim Marshall) which appeared in Volume 40, Issue 3
Chapters © 2009 The Authors
Book compilation © 2009 Philosophy of Education Society of Australasia

Blackwell Publishing was acquired by John Wiley & Sons in February 2007. Blackwell's publishing program has been merged with Wiley's global Scientific, Technical, and Medical business to form Wiley-Blackwell.

Registered Office
John Wiley & Sons Ltd, The Atrium, Southern Gate, Chichester, West Sussex, PO19 8SQ, United Kingdom

Editorial Offices
350 Main Street, Malden, MA 02148-5020, USA
9600 Garsington Road, Oxford, OX4 2DQ, UK
The Atrium, Southern Gate, Chichester, West Sussex, PO19 8SQ, UK

For details of our global editorial offices, for customer services, and for information about how to apply for permission to reuse the copyright material in this book please see our website at www.wiley.com/wiley-blackwell.

Library of Congress Cataloging-in-Publication Data

Academic writing, philosophy, and genre / edited by Michael A. Peters.
    p. cm.
    "Originally published as volume 40, issue 7 of *Educational Philosophy and Theory*, except for chapter 7, Philosophy as Literature by Jim Marshall which appeared in volume 40, issue 3"—T.p. verso.
    Includes bibliographical references and index.
    ISBN 978-1-4051-9400-6 (pbk. : alk. paper) 1. Philosophy—Authorship. I. Peters, Michael A.
    B52.7.A23 2009
    100–dc22

                                                                    2009006560

A catalogue record for this book is available from the British Library.

Set in 10pt Plantin by Graphicraft Limited, Hong Kong
Printed and bound in Malaysia by KHL Printing Co Sdn Bhd

01   2009

Contents

Notes on Contributors

Sarah Allen is an Assistant Professor in the School of English Language and Literature at the University of Northern Colorado in Greeley, CO, where she serves as a Rhetoric and Composition scholar and teacher. Her scholarship, which is informed by Foucault's work on the care of the self, has been focused primarily on the practices of self writing in personal essays. She is most recently working on a book project on imitation practices in writing.

David Gorman is Associate Professor of English at Northern Illinois University. He has published in various formats on the history and theory of literary criticism, including essays, reviews, bibliographies, translations, and entries in reference works. Gorman has also published on the philosophy of language.

James Marshall is Emeritus Professor of Education at The University of Auckland, and Research Professor at The University of North Carolina at Chapel Hill. He has published extensively in Philosophy of Education and recent books include *Michel Foucault; Personal autonomy and education* (1996), and (ed.) *Poststructuralism, Philosophy, Pedagogy* (2004). His major interests at present are in Continental philosophy.

Rob McCormack is at Victoria University, Melbourne, Australia. His PhD deployed Gadamer in order to reframe adult literacy and adult basic education as inheriting the tradition of practical philosophy, not just modernist educational discourses.

Michael A. Peters is Professor of Education at the University of Illinois at Urbana-Champaign. He has degrees in geography, philosophy and education. He previously held a chair as research professor and professor of education at the University of Glasgow (2000–2005) as well as a personal chair at the University of Auckland and adjunct professor of communication studies at the Auckland University of Technology. He is the editor of three international journals: *Educational Philosophy and Theory*; *Policy Futures in Education*; and *E-Learning*. He is also the author or editor of over forty books, including most recently *Global Knowledge Cultures* (2007), *Knowledge Economy, Development and the Future of Higher Education* (2007), *Building Knowledge Cultures: Education in the Age of Knowledge Capitalism* (2006), and *Deconstructing Derrida: Tasks for the New Humanities* (2005). His research interests include educational philosophy, education and public policy, social and political theory.

Thomas E. Peterson is Professor of Italian at the University of Georgia. His primary research interests are in the areas of Italian lyric and epic poetry (Dante, Petrarch, Tasso, Leopardi, Pascoli, the poets of the 20th century) and the Italian novel. His research in educational philosophy has its origins in his study of Vico and Whitehead and the process philosophy tradition; current research seeks to connect the wisdom and practical pedagogy of that tradition to the work of (among others) Dewey, Peirce, Cassirer, Gregory and Mary Catherine Bateson, Francisco Varela and Heinz von Foerster. You may contact him at peterson@uga.edu.

Peter Roberts is Professor of Education at the University of Canterbury in Christchurch, New Zealand. His main areas of teaching expertise are philosophy of education and educational policy studies. His research interests include literature and education, ethics and education, the work of Paulo Freire, and tertiary education policy. Professor Roberts has published widely in international journals. His work has appeared in *Educational Theory*, the *Journal of Philosophy of Education*, *Studies in Philosophy and Education*, *Educational Philosophy and Theory*, the *Journal of Moral Education*, the *British Journal of Educational Studies*, the *Oxford Review of Education*, the *Journal of Educational Thought*, *Interchange*, the *Journal of Transformative Education*, *Studies in Higher Education*, *Policy Futures in Education*, the *International Review of Education*, the *International Journal of Lifelong Education*, and many other journals. His books include (2000) *Education, Literacy and Humanization: Exploring the Work of Paulo Freire* (Westport, CT, Bergin and Garvey), (1999, with Michael Peters) *University Futures and the Politics of Reform* (Palmerston North, Dunmore Press), and (2001, edited with Mark Chambers) *Digital Developments in Higher Education: Theory and Practice* (Cambridge, Taylor Graham Publishing), among others. His forthcoming books are *Neoliberalism, Higher Education and Research* (with Michael Peters, Rotterdam, Sense Publishers), *The Virtues of Openness* (with Michael Peters, Boulder, CO, and London, Paradigm Publishers), and *Uncertainty, Dialogue and Transformation* (Boulder, CO, and London, Paradigm Publishers).

John D. Schaeffer is Professor of English at Northern Illinois University where he teaches courses in the history of rhetoric and Renaissance English literature. He has published articles on these subjects in *PMLA*, *Studies in Philology*, *Rhetorica*, *Rhetoric Society Quarterly*, *Milton Quarterly*, and other journals. His book, *Sensus Communis: Vico, rhetoric, and the limits of relativism* (1990) was published by Duke University Press.

Introduction

Thinking in Fragments; Thinking in Systems

Michael A. Peters

> To know is one thing, merely to believe one knows is another. To know is science, but merely to believe one knows is ignorance.
> —Hippocrates, *Aphorisms*

> Philosophy ought really to be written only as a form of poetry.
> —Ludwig Wittgenstein, *Culture and Value*

Aphoristic Thought

One of the consequences of a materialist and historicist view of discourse and academic writing is that one is inclined also to hold that there is a relationship between the form of thinking and the form of discourse. This is not necessarily a one-way or causative relationship but it does build upon the maxim underlying the linguistic turn—that thought is expressed in language and the sentence, linguistically speaking, constitutes a unit of thought open to the logic of truth-functional value-testing (Peters, 2007). The kind of relationship I am elaborating is provided by the example of aphoristic writing. The genre is an ancient form, from the Greek αφορισμός) (aphorismos) meaning 'to limit' or 'define' and denoting an original thought, a short pithy statement, expressing an evident truth in easily memorable form. Hippocrates' Aphorisms (written 400 B.C.E) provides an early example of the form.[1] He uses the form to state a series of medical observations from which the patient's affliction could be deduced and treatment prescribed.

It belonged to what is commonly called the 'wisdom literature' exemplified in 'sayings' and intended to teach about virtue. These 'sayings' are clearly evident in Biblical wisdom literature such as the *The Book of Job* and *The Book of Proverbs* and also in the Hebraic and Islamic traditions.

The genre was used later by Hesiod, Epitetus, and Plutarch, among others. The form of aphorism was reinvented during the Renaissance where it made use of mnemonic statements. Later the form was embraced by Erasmus, Rochefoucauld, and Pascal who saw in it the basis for a formulation of a moral principle. Dr Johnson that human institution of English letters defined the aphorism as 'a maxim; a precept contracted in a short sentence; an unconnected position.' He favored the form because he thought it could stand by itself and treat a moral topic.

Morson (2003: 409) argues that 'aphorism, dictum, maxim, slogan, witticism, hypothesis, thought, and many other terms for short expressions have no clear definition and are used in contradictory or overlapping ways. Groarke (2007) provides an account of the aphorism as a philosophical genre elucidating the aphorism as an expression of 'aphoristic consciousness,' focusing on Pascal's aphoristic style, and the exegetical issues surrounding his *Pensées*. He demonstrates that aphoristic consciousness in an epistemological sense has been a *topoi* of Western philosophy.

With Dr Johnson in England and with Lichtenberg and later Nietzsche on the Continent the aphorism comes to inaugurate a moment or figure of thought that is more philosophical than literary (Fritz Mautner; J.P. Stern). It is this tradition that informs the gnomic statement and formulations of Karl Kraus and also the innovative ness of the thought experiment. In this context I am drawn immediately to Ludwig Wittgenstein and his style of philosophizing based on an understanding of the genre of aphorism as it motivates his method of composition (Peters & Burbules, 2002).

Wittgenstein's style owes a great deal to the great German aphorist Georg Christoph Lichtenberg (Wright, 1982). Kimball (2002) argues that 'Lichtenberg's influence on Wittgenstein's work went deeper than mere content: the gnomic form of the *Tractatus* and *Philosophical Investigations* owes a great deal to the example of Lichtenberg's aphorisms.' While Kimball notices the connection and its significance for Wittgenstein he really does not grasp the significance of Lichtenberg for Wittgenstein's style of composition. In Peters and Burbules (2002) we argued:

> All students of Wittgenstein who have grown up with the Wittgenstein 'mythology' know certain fundamental things about him and his work: that although Wittgenstein wrote a great deal he published very little in his own lifetime; that everything he wrote became part of a complex process of composition, passing from first or early drafts to finished work, through a number of phases; that what he wrote is difficult, if not impossible, to distinguish from what he said; and that what he did not write or say—what could only be *shown*—was at least as important as what he said and wrote. Each of these features, although perhaps obvious and familiar, requires further elucidation for the light they shine on Wittgenstein's styles.

> The scope and character of Wittgenstein's literary *Nachlass*, the so-called 'Wittgenstein Papers', fall into three main groups: (a) the manuscripts (78), consisting of two *strata* of writings 'first drafts' and 'more finished versions'; (b) the typescripts (34) which were dictated or prepared by Wittgenstein himself; and (c) verbatim records of dictations (8) to colleagues or pupils (Von Wright, 1969: 485–86). In addition, von Wright mentions two further groups: the notes, more or less verbatim, of Wittgenstein's conversations and lectures; and his correspondence. Already, one might note that there is something extraordinary about the amount he wrote, most of which was never published in his lifetime. He agonised over the form and composition of his work and he developed

very complex methods of composition. He comments in *Culture and Value* that when he is thinking about a topic he 'jump[s] about all round it': 'Forcing my thoughts into an ordered sequence is a torment for me ... . I squander an unspeakable amount of effort making an arrangement of my thoughts which may have no value at all' (CV, 28e). Von Wright (1969: 503) refers to the 'layers of composition' of his work and describes the process of composition as one that involved dictation to a typist from a finished manuscript in which he would change and add words and sentences.

His method of composition based on the aphorisms was first to recognize the fragmentary nature of thought that comes to us in fragments and insights, rather than from a sustained effort of thinking. These flashes of insight then needed to be recorded in notebooks. Their statement then was worked on and together they became the raw material for a kind of composition process that attempted to provide a 'natural order'.

Encyclopedic thought[2]

The word 'Encyclopedia' comes from Greek *enkyklopaideia*. It means 'the circle of the education,' or a complete system of learning—if we take the expression literally. It is useful to think of the word and its original Greek meaning because it reminds us that the first encyclopedias, and the ordinary meaning of the word, did not draw any hard and fast distinctions between 'philosophy' and 'knowledge' and 'education.' Indeed, for over 2000 years from the point of its classical inception, through its history of transformations in the medieval, modern and postmodern periods, the encyclopedia has remained an exemplary pedagogical system designed to provide summaries of existing scholarship—often both the meanings and referents of words and concepts—in an accessible language and format for particular audiences.

Of all pedagogical systems and reference works—such as dictionaries, almanacs, gazetteers, atlases and directories—the encyclopedia was the only one to aim at a total comprehensive and self-contained system, although there was no one set of principles guiding the method for classification of entries or arrangement of contents. Classifications varied considerably in the period before the alphabetical arrangement of entries was introduced through a standardization that came with printing, reflecting the working epistemologies of the age and the evolution of disciplines and the formation of knowledges. Classical and medieval encyclopedias often classified contents arranged according to subject. Pliny's *Historia naturalis*, perhaps the highpoint of the classical encyclopedia, organized its contents by reference to the subjects of government, geography, zoology, medicine, history and practical matters. Contemporary philosophies were discussed impartially without any indication of personal preference. This 'objective' approach was not employed again until the 19th century. Those encyclopedists like St. Isidore of Seville, who were educated in the classical tradition, gave priority to the liberal arts and medicine. An important stage in the history of the encyclopedia was reached with Francis

Bacon's structure, which was arranged 'scientifically' into 'External Nature', 'Man' and 'Man's Action on Nature' based upon his empiricism. Bacon's project was to provide a comprehensive outline of the entire corpus of human knowledge. His form of classification was so influential that 130 years later Denis Diderot acknowledged his debt to Bacon in his *Encyclopédie* and Coleridge in his *Encyclopedia Metropolitiana*, impressed with Bacon, drew up a different table consisting of the five main classes of the 'pure' sciences, both formal (philology, logic, mathematics) and real (metaphysics, morals, theology), mixed and applied sciences (mixed: mechanics, hydrostatics, pneumatics, optics, astronomy; and applied: experimental philosophy, the fine arts, the useful arts, natural history, application of natural history); biography and history; miscellaneous and lexicographical; and an analytical index.

For both Diderot and Coleridge the encyclopedia revealed the structure of knowledge—its unity and its principles of harmony—and this logical structure was deemed necessary for its elucidation and ease of learning. The encyclopedia was also seen as an instrument to think methodically. From the earliest of times, the encyclopedia was considered an instrument for the pursuit of truth, dedicated to the improvement of mankind. Knowledge, in its vast comprehensiveness, arranged or organized into its 'natural' branches or disciplines and articulated into a giant system covering its full scope, was considered necessary for the good of society. In this sense then the early medieval and ecclesiastical encyclopedias, such as Vincent of Beavais's *Speculum Majus* ('The Great Mirror') or Domenico Bandini's *Fons Memorabilium Universi* ('The Source of Noteworthy facts of the Universe'), considerably predated the Enlightenment's emphasis on the relation between 'truth', 'knowledge', 'philosophy', 'education' and 'enlightenment', and 'the good society'.

Diderot and D'Alembert developed their underlying epistemology governing their Encyclopédie under the influence of Locke and Condillac: a rational and positivistic classification of existing knowledge based on the assumption of the unity of theory and praxis. Diderot planned to provide complete alphabetical treatment of the whole field of human knowledge from the standpoint of the 'Enlightenment' and the contributors included Montesquieu, Voltaire, Rousseau, Turgot and Condorcet. The 28 volumes of the *Encyclopédie* completed between 1751–72 were not simply a repository of human knowledge but also a polemic from the viewpoint of the French Enlightenment and as such included a strong emphasis on democracy and equality, and a kind of tolerance of philosophical views that were essentially subversive of the established order.

The doors of the Modern Age opened, when the World walked by larger steps, and the division between 'education' and 'philosophy' was made definitively. The French philosophers, perhaps against themselves, wanted to hold on to something like a classical Paideia. But if this wasn't possible—and if some scholars already knew that it wasn't possible anymore because knowledges began to split and fragment into its professional specialties, then they, the French philosophers, would work in order to hold into a circle, even in its arrested form, the Paideia—education, in its classical expression.

What does Encyclopedia mean in a world in which a big gap exists between 'philosophy' and 'knowledge' and 'education'? What does Encyclopedia mean in a world in which all this is a reality and in spite of the traditional gaps and disciplinary separations, the Internet becomes a great dominion? This is mainly a sociological problem; perhaps, also a philosophical problem. But also surely a social and existential problem. The sociological difficulty is something for the sociologists. The social and existential problem is, in this case, something very complex and dangerous, perhaps. Yet the philosophical problem shows itself to be one capable of rational discussion and debate. And when we come to discuss the Net as philosophers—its effects on knowledge and the disciplines, its manner of organization and classifying knowledge—we must be self-reflexively consistent; we must, at least, attempt to understand cyberspace in its applications to our own case.

In a few short years, the Internet has gone from being a specialist site for a few scientists and engineers to a place—a soft and almost infinitely flexible architecture—which incorporates a staggering variety of spaces: not just information exchange or reference banks or dictionaries but a vast conglomeration of different spaces, teeming with activity. The Internet, perhaps like the encyclopedia of old, now speaks to implicit knowledge formations, hybrid discourses, personal homepages that approve the existential conditions for aesthetically transforming oneself, chatgroups, bargain basements, advertising, new businesses and the whole vista of bookish elements now chaotically 'shelved' alongside video clips, images and other non-textual items. For the first time, the desire of the medieval or Enlightenment encyclopedists of bringing together the entire scope and corpus of human knowledge and information looks more than a possibility rather than simply a historical reflection of the vanity of a bygone age.

Yet some philosophers complain that the Internet promotes a collapse of knowledge into information or simply data, and they inform us that none of the three conditions of the traditional Platonic definition of knowledge as justified true belief are met: for information there does not need to be a belief condition, a truth condition or a justification condition. On one view this dangerous conflation imperils us, on another it promotes new discourses and new possibilities for dialogue. Of course, the reality is that there is both knowledge and information, and also cases where knowledge has been reduced to information, but there are also new kinds of discourse and the radical concordance of image, music, text and video. Our encyclopedia is, of course, not a compendium of knowledge items: it does not pretend to be the last word. Indeed, we would argue that the Internet and electronic space encourages a kind of philosophical pluralism for the same spatial limitations no longer exist: in our encyclopedia there is room for multiple entries and plural interpretations. And 'dynamic' encyclopedias—even specialist ones like the Encyclopedia of Philosophy of Education—promote the possibility of an infinite revisability. We do not hope to complete 'the circle of learning' or to develop a rationalist system that effects a kind of closure, but we do hope that the Encyclopedia can, perhaps, widen the circle, to include more contributions and to admit many more learners and readers into the circle than was ever imagined by our encyclopedist predecessors.

The essays in this monograph pick up on various aspects of themes to do with philosophy, genre and academic writing especially as they manifest themselves in higher education. They explore the dimensions of relationships among philosophy and literature, philosophy and genre, academic writing, and the wider issues associated with the politics and philosophy of writing.

Notes

1. For the full text see http://classics.mit.edu/Hippocrates/aphorisms.html trans. by Francis Adams.
2. This section is based on Peters & Gharadelli (1999).

References

Groarke, L. (2007) Philosophy as Inspiration: Blaise Pascal and the Epistemology of Aphorisms, *Poetics Today*, 28(3): 393–441.

Kimball, R. (2002) G. C. Lichtenberg: a 'spy on humanity'. On the Aphorist. *The New Criterion*, 20, at http://www.newcriterion.com/articles.cfm/lichtenberg-kimball-1963

Morson, G. S. (2003) The Aphorism: Fragments from the Breakdown of Reason, *New Literary History*, 34(3) Summer: 409–429.

Peters, M. A. & Ghiraldelli, P. Jnr. (1999) The Encyclopedia of Philosophy of Education: Encyclopaideia, Philosopedia, or Macropedagogy? At http://www.vusst.hr/ENCYCLOPAEDIA/main.htm

Peters, M. A. & Burbules, N. (2002) Wittgenstein/Styles/Pedagogy, *Theory & Science*, 3, 1: http://www.icaap.org/iuicode?105.3.1.x.

Peters, M. A. (2007) Kinds of Thinking, Styles of Reasoning, *Educational Philosophy and Theory*, Special Issue on critical thinking, Mark Mason (Ed.), 39(5).

Quivy, M. and Romanski, P. (2007) *Dreaming Aphorisms, Cercles: Interdisciplinary Journal of Anglophone Literature*, Occasional Papers Series, 9: 103–109.

Wright, G. H. (1982) 'Wittgenstein in Relation to his Times'. In: B. McGuinness (Ed.) *Wittgenstein and His Times*, Oxford, Basil Blackwell.

Wright, G. H. 'Ludwig Wittgenstein: A Biographical Sketch' in his *Wittgenstein* (Oxford: Blackwell, 1982), 15–34.

1

Academic Writing, Genres and Philosophy

MICHAEL A. PETERS

> Plato had to distinguish what he was doing from all other discursive
> practices that laid claim to wisdom. It is for this reason that, in dialogue
> after dialogue, Plato deliberately set out to define and defend a new and
> quite peculiar mode of living and thinking. This alone, he claimed
> deserved the title of 'philosophy'.
>
> —Andrea Wilson Nightingale, *Genres in Dialogue:*
> *Plato and the Construct of Philosophy*

> Philosophy is expressed—and for this reason is fully made real—within a
> definite literary genre; and it must be emphasized that prior to this
> expression it did not exist except in a precarious way or, rather, only as
> intention and attempt. Philosophy is thus intrinsically bound to the
> literary genre, not into which it is poured, but, we would do better to say,
> in which it is incarnated.
>
> —Julián Marías, 'Literary Genres in Philosophy'

> Philosophical writing, as a genre, redefined itself in the mid-to-late 17th
> century when philosophers decided they needed to define words rather
> than things. Because philosophy then could not be separated from science
> generally, the 1660 Royal Society helped 'professionalize' language in this
> way. It stole much fire from literary writing. It also forced literary genres
> into being because, after all, poets were no longer writing about either
> things (as encyclopedists did) or words (an expertise philosophers laid
> new claim to). What was the poet's 'profession', then, but writing
> 'drama', or 'novels', or 'essays'?
>
> —Ian Lancashire, 'Lexicographical Meditations: A sense of genre'

Genres and Philosophy

Philosophy possesses both oral and written forms of expression. We might as well
say it also possesses the practices, norms and rituals that comprise an institution
and define the rules of a discourse. It is practiced in a variety of pedagogical
contexts whose oral forms have been with us for a long time, remarkably assuming
a kind of performative stability: the dialogue, the symposium, the address, and,

perhaps, more recently, the lecture, the seminar, the oral defense, the tutorial. Yet philosophy's pedagogies—at least those parts predominately oral and performative, if it makes sense to separate them—have remained hidden by their familiarity, to make a Wittgensteinian point. Their very familiarity is what makes them difficult to problematize as they are the taken-for-granted forms, hardly recognizable in terms of 'forms' that order our academic and institutional life. This is not to deny the intermingling of oral and written forms or the way that they reinforce each other in various sequences for different purposes, audiences and occasions. The oral forms of philosophy and academic expression have a history that is difficult to chart or even to begin to problematize.

Philosophical texts display a variety of literary forms: there are many different philosophical genres that have developed over the years which are peculiar to and transcend their age: letters, the treatise, the thesis, the confession, the meditation, the allegory, the essay, the soliloquy, the symposium, the consolation, the commentary, the disputation, and the dialogue, to name a few. These forms of philosophy have conditioned and become the basis of academic writing (and assessment) within both the university and higher education more generally. Within pedagogical environments, these forms take on new force as part of institutional and scholarship life, patched together into a set of practices that determines academic rituals and routines of the everyday. Some forms and their associated 'styles' (both written and performative) are 'individual' and some are group styles and truly collective. Since the cultural, linguistic (discursive), and practice turns of the 1970s and in subsequent decades greater attention has been paid to the relations between academic writing, genres and philosophy, and also to questions of style, genre, form and their historicity and materiality. These are themes strongly pursued by some of the leading philosophers of the age, including, Stanley Cavell and Jacques Derrida on the relations of philosophy and literature, and Richard Rorty on post-analytic (narrative) genres in philosophy or 'philosophy as a kind of writing' as he put it in a famous essay on Derrida (Rorty, 1982).[1] There is a certain materiality of writing and of its academic forms that for philosophy and history (and other characteristic forms of the humanities) pose a peculiar relation to time—to its claims to universality and its ability to transcend the local and the particular.

Since Northrop Frye (1957) originally used the theory of genre to differentiate types of literature and to consider whether a work may be considered to belong to a class of related works it has been received in a range of related fields including history, academic writing, and film and television studies.[2] Bakhtin (1986) was an early innovator who formulated an influential theory about speech genres and is justly famous for his account of the *bildungsroman* and its significance in the history of realism. (His works only became available in English translation after 1968.) Only recently has the concept of genre been applied to philosophy and to the question of philosophical form, especially by thinkers like Derrida (1980) in 'The Law of Genre' where he initiates and investigates the uses and limits of genre as mode of classification and analysis. Derrida argues that particular texts participate in rather than belong to certain genres by showing that the 'mark of genre' is not itself a member of a genre or type. He ends his essay by drawing attention to the act of classification itself and the way in which taxonomies themselves require careful scrutiny as to their history.[3]

Derrida's original dissertation concerned the form of the thesis. He completed his Thèse d'État in 1980 and the work was subsequently published in English translation as 'The Time of a Thesis—Punctuations'. Not only did it self-consciously provide autobiographical insertions in the philosophical tradition as part of the defense of his thesis at the Sorbonne but also his introduction to Husserlian phenomenology at the time of writing. The thesis form itself and the kind of academic writing associated with it quickly became an object of criticism: 'The very idea of a thetic presentation, of positional or oppositional logic, the idea of a position ... was one of the essential parts of the system that was under deconstructive criticism' (Derrida, 1983, p. 35). Inevitably, the thesis form and its historical accretions (and the dissertation) are simultaneously forms of academic writing and knowledge. The materiality of the form becomes central as we begin to reflect on the history of the form and its interrelationships with the doctorate *per se* and with PhD educational practices, with the oral defense, and with acceptable forms of criticism.

Another aspect of Derrida's (1974) work in *Of Grammatology* is also useful, especially the historical and metaphysical principles that determine the place of writing versus speech, and the way in which the speech/writing opposition can be mapped onto a series of ideologically loaded pairs that are constitutive of modern Western culture: speech/writing; natural/artificial; spontaneous/constructed; original/copy; interior to the mind/exterior to the mind; intuitive/learned. I do not have the time to track out all that follows from establishing a science of writing in Derrida's terms or indeed how scientificity (objectivity, memory etc.) itself is an aspect of writing and a condition of a certain episteme and age of the university. Derrida teaches us that the Western philosophical tradition has denigrated writing as an inferior copy of the spoken word: speech is more immediate and transparent and draws on interior consciousness, whereas writing is dead and abstract. The written word loses its spiritual connection to the self and the written word, untethered from the speaking subject, is cast adrift from personality and intentionality.

In the English-speaking world, Berel Lang's work in the early 1980s was path breaking on the poetics of philosophical discourse. As he says in the Preface to *Philosophy and the Art of Writing* (1983) 'philosophical discourse is a form of making as well as of knowing', 'the process of making ... is a version of praxis or doing', and 'the role of a persona ... within the work is a condition of its intelligibility' (p. 9). As he goes on to explain in the first chapter, while 'the history of Western philosophy is predominantly a history of written texts ... philosophers have lived in that history and looked back at it as if a dependence on such unusual and complex artifacts had nothing to do with the work of philosophy itself' (p. 19).

The recent collection *Literary Form, Philosophical Content: Historical Studies in Philosophical Genre* (Lavery, 2008) is based on these insights and sits within a line of thinking strongly influenced by Berel Lang who provides the Epilogue. In 'The Ethics of Style in Philosophical Discourse' Lang examines forms of writing in which the author addresses the reader as an equal or as an authority. The first two essays, 'Platonic Preludes' by Dorter and Gallop, investigate by turn skepticism and Plato's student-teacher dramas and the specificity of the Platonic dialogue. The other essays in the section 'Beyond Dialogue' take on Aesop as a form of philosophical biography and philosophy as prayer, commentary, disputation, political manual, miscellany, polemics, lecture and science fiction. As the subtitle suggests this collection provides a set of historical studies in philosophical genre. In one sense, the form of an edited collection ideally suits this topic and this set of essays advances the field considerably by providing a comprehensive demonstration of the variety of philosophical genres. The introductory essay carefully outlines scholarly interest in philosophical genre. As the editors indicate: 'Genre can function as an interpretive tool for elucidating details of a work's meaning and purpose and ... it can function as an analytic tool for unstitching a work at its seams' (p. 6).

Hayden White (2003), the US historian strongly influenced by Foucault who worked out of a narratology perspective, has worked on genre ambiguities in relation to history and literary theory, and the problem of its 'resistance to theory': 'Genre', he argues, 'is a construction of thought more metaphysical than scientific in its founding formulation' (p. 600). Genre and genre-fication are open to change and destabilization as new hybrids flower.

Berkenkotter and Huckin (1995) use the term 'genre knowledge' to refer to 'an individual's repertoire of situationally appropriate responses to recurrent situations— from immediate encounters to distanced communication through the medium of print, and more recently, the electronic media'. They argue:

> Our thesis is that genres are inherently dynamic rhetorical structures that can he manipulated according to the conditions of use, and that genre knowledge is therefore best conceptualized as a form of situated cognition embedded in disciplinary activities. (p. 3)

Their combined intention is to study 'the textual character of disciplinary communication' by examining both 'the situated actions of writers, and the communicative systems in which disciplinary actors participate'. They state:

> From this perspective we propose that what microlevel studies of actors' situated actions frequently depict as individual processes, can also be interpreted (from the macrolevel) as communicative acts within a discursive network or system. Genre is the concept that enables us to envision the interpenetration of process and system in disciplinary communication. (p. x)

Their theoretical view is based on grounded theory in the sense that they have engaged in the systematic observation of the professional activities of individual writers. But they also explain that their theoretical framework is informed by Gidden's structuration theory in sociology, rhetorical studies, interpretive anthro-pology, ethnomethodology, Bakhtin's theory of speech genres, Vygotsky's theory of ontogenesis, and Russian activity theory 'as it has shaped the movement in U.S. psychology called situated or everyday cognition' (p. 3).

Berkenkotter and Huckin (1995, p. 4) highlight features of the genre concept as follows:

1) *Dynamism*. Genres are dynamic rhetorical forms that are developed from actors' responses to recurrent situations and that serve to stabilize experience and give its coherence and meaning. Genres change over time in response to their users' sociocognitive needs.
2) *Situatedness*. Our knowledge of genres is derived from and embedded in our participation in the communicative activities of daily and professional life. As such, genre knowledge is a form of 'situated cognition' that continues to develop as we participate in the activities of the ambient culture.
3) *Form and content*. Genre knowledge embraces both form and content, including a sense of what content is appropriate to a particular purpose in a particular situation at a particular point of time.
4) *Duality of structure*. As we draw on genre rules to engage in professional activities, we *constitute* social structures (in professional, institutional, and organizational contexts) and simultaneously *reproduce* these structures.
5) *Community ownership*. Genre conversations signal a discourse on community's norms, epistemology, ideology, and social ontology.

Their approach in terms of situated cognition provides the means for the investigation of 'the recent evolution of the scientific journal article, the primary genre for the dissemination of new scientific knowledge' (p. 27). They conclude.

1) During the past half century, scientists have come under increasing pressure from the information explosion and, therefore, have been accessing and reading specialized journal articles in an increasingly selective manner, searching for the most newsworthy information; this reading behavior is not unlike that of ordinary people accessing and reading newspaper articles.
2) To accommodate this reading behavior, the genre conventions used in scientific journals have undergone gradual changes.
3) The dynamism that can be observed in this diachronic textual evidence of the past half century reflects changes in the way the scientific community goes about its work. (p. 42)

They investigate novelty and intertextuality in a biologists' experimental article suggesting 'You are what you cite' (chapter 3), and 'Sites of Contention; Sites of Negotiation: Textual dynamics of peer review in the construction of scientific knowledge' (chapter 4) as well as scientific forums (chapter 5) and gatekeeping at conventions, before focusing on 'An Apprenticeship Tale of a Doctoral Student' (chapter 7). In a subsequent chapter Berkenkotter and Huckin (1995) apply their method to learning to speak and to write and to special classes of genres known as curriculum, pedagogical, or classroom genres. Their approach to genre knowledges as forms of mediated cognition thus provide a method and approach to understanding practices of academic writing (see also Bhatia, 2004).

These themes and related questions have been pursued in relation to geopolitics of writing (see Canagarajah, 2002) and to new hybrid electronic forms of academic discourse. This book takes these questions, in part, as central and significant to understanding and investigating pedagogy, and the history and future of its institutions.

Academic Writing and a Brief History of the Essay

> 'Tis the custom of pedagogues to be eternally thundering in their pupil's ears, as they were pouring into a funnel, while the business of the pupil is only to repeat what the others have said: now I would have a tutor to correct this error, and, that at the very first, he should, according to the capacity he has to deal with, put it to the test, permitting his pupil himself to taste things, and of himself to discern and choose them, sometimes opening the way to him, and sometimes leaving him to open it for himself; that is, I would not have him alone to invent and speak, but that he should also hear his pupil speak in turn.
>
> —Montaigne, 'Of the Education of Children', 1575

Academic writing takes many different standard forms based upon the ubiquitous essay, and research paper. The academic essay now most often takes the form of the journal article that includes an abstract and key words and varies in length anything from 5–10 thousand words with one or more authors. The concept of the essay and its form comes from the French *essai* and derives from the French infinitive *essayer*, 'to try' or 'to attempt' but also from the Latin *exigere*, 'to drive out, to try, or to examine'. Montaigne's *Essais*, published in two volumes in 1580, are often held to be the first and definitive examples of the form.[4] Montaigne, inspired by Plutarch's *Moral Works*, used the term to characterize these essays as 'attempts' or 'trials' to express his thoughts adequately in writing. Montaigne certainly popularized the genre of the essay as a literary form. His stated goal in 'The author to the reader' is to describe man and himself with total frankness:

> *I desire thereun to be delineated in mine own genuine, simple and ordinarie fashion, without contention, art or study; for it is myselfe I pourtray. My imperfections shall thus be read to the life, and my naturall forme discerned, so farre-forth as publike reverence hath permitted me. For if my fortune had beene to have lived among those nations which yet are said to live under the sweet liberty of Nature's first and uncorrupted lawes, I assure thee, I would most willingly have pourtrayed myselfe fully and naked.*
>
> (http://www.uoregon.edu/~rbear/montaigne/)

The essay is an elastic form at least before its mutation into the primary academic genre. It has referred to works in verse such as Alexander Pope's *An Essay of Man* and as such its philosophical content precedes its literary form as a brief, concentrated and systematic reflection on a single topic written in a formal register. The form that flowered in the Renaissance under Montaigne was adopted by Francis Bacon as quintessential of the new science adequate to expressing new knowledge and truths of the new empirical science.[5] Bacon's essays are, as he says, basically 'civil and moral counsels' that express current views in an epigrammatic, assertive and aphoristic way. In the golden age of rationalism Robert Boyle utilized the essay form as a basis for reflecting on the relations between religion and science. His *Certain Physiological Essays* (1661) was seen as adopting a new form of discourse suited to the contents of the new science. Later the form at least in title was adopted by Locke and Malthus in their extended reflections—*An Essay Concerning Human Understanding* and *An Essay on the Principle of Population* culminating in the two important periodicals established by Joseph Addison & Richard Steele in the early decades of the 18th century. *The Tatler* (1709–11) and *The Spectator* (1711–12) discussed the range of current events mingled with snippets of literature, and gossip and often written in a highly ironic style.

The literary form became a pedagogical form with its adoption as a formal means of evaluating student's comprehension and writing where they are asked to explain or comment on a topic or proposition in the form of an essay. In this process of institutionalization the form of the essays underwent a pedagogical formalization, moving away from its literary characteristics to emphasis a logical and factual treatment of a topic in an objective register that until recently discouraged the voice, views or identification of the identity of the author and, in particular, the use of the first person singular. There is more pedagogical history revealed in the transmutation of the essay genre from its literary to its formal pedagogical form than can be imagined.

The academic article based on the essay cannot be separated from the institutions of the academic periodical or journal which has a relatively short history beginning (to all intents and purposes) with *The Philosophical Transactions of the Royal Society* in 1665 with Henry Oldenburg as its first editor and featuring his correspondence with Europe's leading scientists. The academic journal article, which is still the main form of scientific communication, is also defined in part by a set of evolving academic practices that includes peer review. With the Internet the future of the journal is undergoing a huge transformation especially as databases, manuals, reference works, guides, indexes, and full-text articles became available in public knowledge banks.

The History of Scientific Communication

The history of scientific communication demonstrates that the typical form of the scientific article presented in print-based journals in essay form is a result of development over two centuries beginning in the 17th century with the emergence of learned societies and cooperation among scientists. *Journal des Sçavans*, the first journal, was published in Paris in 1665 (Fjällbrant, 1997) as a 12 page quarto pamphlet, appearing only a few months before the *Philosophical Transactions of the Royal Society*, the oldest journal in continuous production.[6] The development of the journal and scientific norms of cooperation, forms of academic writing and the norm of peer review was part and parcel of the institutionalization of science, first with the development of the model of the Royal Society that was emulated elsewhere in Europe and the US, and then later institutionalization received a strong impetus from the emergence of the modern research university beginning with the establishment of the University of Berlin in 1810 in the reforms of Humboldt. This institutionalization of science necessarily also was a part of the juridical-legal system of writing that grew up around the notion of a professional scientist and academic, the notion of the academic author, the idea of public science or research, the ownership of ideas and academic recognition for the author who claimed originality for a discovery, set of results or piece of scholarship (Kaufer & Carley, 1993).

The history of scientific communication, even in the post-war period, is a mammoth undertaking where technological developments and the new paradigm of open knowledge production seem to outstrip our capacity to give an adequate account of them. There is so much experimentation by way of new electronic journals launched and new projects being established that it is near impossible to document even the range in its diversity let alone theorize its main characteristics and implications for modes of scientific communication. One source, perhaps the most comprehensive, provides a bibliography on scholarly electronic publishing that runs to 1,400 items in English under such categories as: economic issues; electronic books & texts; electronic serials; general works; legal issues; library issues; new publishing models; publisher issues; repositories, e-prints and AOI (Bailey, 2006; see also 2001).

The history of electronic scientific communication itself is now nearly 20 years old if we date the process from the appearance of the first electronic journals. The electronic revolution of those first utopian years in the early 1990s with predictions of the collapse of the traditional print-based system, the demise of academic publishers, and the replacement by electronic journals has not yet come to pass. As Valauskas (1997) argues 'electronic scholarly journals differentiate themselves from printed scholarly journals by accelerated peer review, combined with mercurial production schemes ... The sheer interactive nature of digital journals ... and the ability to access the complete archives of a given title on a server make that sort of publishing a significant departure from the long established traditions of print'. He concludes 'Electronic scholarly journals are indeed different from traditional print scholarly journals, but not as radically different as some would argue. They are different in terms of process, but not in terms of the ancient traditions of peer review and verification'.

The form, style and economics of scientific communication were to undergo another set of changes to their socio-technical ecology and infrastructure. The pre-history of the emergence of electronic forms of scientific communication can be traced back at least to Ted Nelson's notion of 'hypertext' which he coined in 1963 and went on to develop as a hypertext system. Some account of the impact of computers on writing is required including the shift from: literacy to orality and the way that computers re-introduce oral characteristics into writing; linearity to connectivity; fixity to fluidity; and passivity to interactivity (Ferris, 2002). Jay David Bolter's (1991) *Writing Space: The computer, hypertext and the history of writing* is the seminal text that explores the computer's place in the history of symbolic (textual) media. The consequences of the networking of science and culture have yet to be worked through fully yet certainly as Bolter points out the new definition of literacy is synonymous with computer literacy and while it is the case that the computer signifies the end of traditional print literacy it does not signify the end of literacy. The Web has now spawned a whole set of new media genres and forms and the Internet has been accepted into education enthusiastically and in a way that previous technologies like television were not. We have not begun to identify systematically the way these new media forms and the development of visual literacy have and will impact upon scientific communication but already there have been some telling signs (see Woolgar, 2000; Nentwich, 2003).

Standardizing Academic Writing

Academic writing also employs standard pedagogical forms of the dissertation and the thesis and the normal fare of academic life is based upon the conference paper. Also in this regard we can mention the book chapter, book review, the translation, the resume, the explication, as well as the academic monograph itself. In addition, pedagogical forms of academic writing include the reading list, the 'handout' as well as numerous forms that include encyclopedic works and other summaries of knowledge, anthologies, catalogues, experiments, and even forms of data collection.

'Academic writing' as a theme, topic or field most often appears in manuals, guides, or programs that purport to teach its various forms or genres through the stipulation of general rules or tips focusing on essay writing. In this form of pedagogy the emphasis falls very much on 'the practical' or practice, offering advice about stages of the writing process (planning and organizing the essay through to final copy), sometimes focusing on its constituent elements of paragraphs or sentences. Sometimes it includes a preliminary introduction to types of academic writing, the development of a 'writing style', grammar, punctuation and composition, and advice on following a system of referencing. On the whole this pedagogical tendency is very much 'hands-on' and directed toward a number of values concerning clarity, access, elegance, simplicity, economy and communication that are implied though rarely questioned or even considered. The emphasis falls squarely on developing technique through examples, checklists, exercises, samples, the exposure of fallacies, practice workshops, and guidelines that often include implicit reference to the extra-textual: the nature of scientific objectivity, impartiality, and truth; argumentation and the rules of evidence; documentation and the provision of examples; the institution of quotation, citation and referencing; the legality of the writing system especially in relation to plagiarism.

In the best programs there is an 'integrated' approach that combines writing with 'foundations of discourse', rhetoric, reading, criticism, and creative as well as academic writing. These programs may also be based upon 'oral and written communication' emphasizing its various forms, especially its newer media forms that mix image, text and sound. A number also pay close attention to a research-orientation, thesis or dissertation writing in relation to publishing generally yet without much discussion of the history of academic publishing, the emergence of journals, or the contemporary political economy of publishing. In these programs and within academia generally there are competing standards of what constitutes 'good writing' that refer to a set of values and assumptions on the relation of language, truth and logic that go largely unquestioned.

As David Russell (2002) demonstrates, before the 1870s writing was taught as ancillary to speaking, and that, as a result, formal writing instruction was essentially training in handwriting, the mechanical process of transcribing sound to visual form. Russell examines academic writing, its origins and its teaching, from a broad institutional perspective investigating the history of little-studied genres of student writing such as the research paper, lab report, and essay examination and tracing the effects of increasing specialization on writing instruction. Today writing, especially in the US, has burgeoned into 'college composition' with a huge range of courses devoted to specialties like 'developmental writing', 'college composition', 'English composition', 'report writing for ...', and writing in various disciplines. Certainly, as Russell notes, two new ideals of academic life, research and utilitarian service, shaped writing instruction into its modern forms.

'Bad Writing'

The issue of 'bad writing' within academia has become a feature of the attack on postmodernism and the culture wars. Denis Dutton (http://www.denisdutton.com/), an American-born New Zealand academic and philosopher of art who teaches at the University of Canterbury and is the editor of *Philosophy and Literature* and the web-based *Arts & Letters Daily* (http://www.aldaily.com/), holds an annual bad writing contest sponsored by his journal. As Dutton (1999) explains in *The Wall Street Journal*:

> Having spent the past 23 years editing a scholarly journal, Philosophy and Literature, I have come to know many lucid and lively academic writers. But for every superb stylist there are a hundred whose writing is no better than adequate—or just plain awful. (http://www.denisdutton.com/language_crimes.htm)

People are encouraged to send in a sentence or two from a published work and typically some seventy entries are sent. Dutton himself and his co-editors of *Philosophy and Literature* are the judges. Round Three (1997) announced Fredric Jameson as the prime sinner; Round Four (1998) nominated Judith Butler and Homi Bhabha as the main culprits. (The competition, it seems, was an annual event from 1996 to 1999.)

The issue is an important one. What constitutes 'good' academic writing is a critical issue that *implies* a theory of literature. Unfortunately Dutton and his editors treat the topic with irony—the competition in reality is a thinly-disguised ideological attack upon the influence of postmodernism and poststructuralism on literary theory and by contrast, also a reactive defense of modernism, rationalism, humanism and 'plain writing'. It is interesting that of the criticisms against 'theory'— read 'poststructuralism'—a number of attacks have resorted to 'humor', satire or irony rather than a full theoretical or argumentative engagement. This is true of the so-called Sokal affair and 'the postmodern generator'.[7] The same intensity and acrimony was directed against Derrida in May 1992 when 20 analytic philosophers from ten countries wrote a letter to the editor of *The Times* (published 9 May) to protest and to intervene in a debate that occurred at Cambridge University over whether Jacques Derrida should be allowed to receive an honorary degree.[8] The signatories, none of whom were faculty at Cambridge, laid two very serious charges against Derrida: that his work 'does not meet accepted standards of clarity and rigour' and that he is not a philosopher. In elaborating these two charges, they argued, first, that while Derrida has shown 'considerable originality' (based upon a number of 'tricks' and 'gimmicks') he has, at the same time, stretched 'the normal forms of academic scholarship beyond recognition', employed 'a written style that defies comprehension', brought contemporary French philosophy into disrepute, and offered nothing but assertions that are either 'false or trivial' in a series of 'attacks upon the values of reason, truth and scholarship'. Second, they submitted, the fact that the influence of his work has been 'almost entirely in fields outside philosophy' was sufficient grounds for casting doubt on his suitability as a candidate for an honorary degree in philosophy.

How much of this blind prejudice is bound up with a lack of understanding of Derrida's project and his writing? The signatories did not seem to realize that 'clarity' in philosophical discourse also has its history and that 'normal forms of academic scholarship' have become 'normalised' or institutionalized and are in the process of changing again, especially in response to the rise of the electronic journal. The use of 'normal' here betrays a politics of philosophy writing and a deep history of the politics of writing in philosophy that stills embraces the false dichotomy of analytic and Continental philosophy in its material forms and perpetuates the myth of a universal form of writing and the dream of a universal form of language called philosophy.

Notes

1. See also Rorty's 'Philosophy as a Transitional Genre' at http://mitpress.mit.edu/books/chapters/0262025671chap1.pdf.
2. For an account 'Development of the Genre Concept' see Leon Breure (2001).
3. See Daniel Chandler's *Introduction to Genre Theory* which while oriented to fiction and film, provides a series of nice observations of the philosophy of taxonomy.
4. See Montaigne's *Essays* (1575) translated by Charles Cotton at http://oregonstate.edu/instruct/phl302/texts/montaigne/m-essays_contents.html. See also the original translation by John Florio of the three books at http://www.uoregon.edu/~rbear/montaigne/ first published in 1603. The e-text is prepared by Ben R. Schneider, Lawrence University, Wisconsin.
5. See *The Complete Essays* of Francis Bacon at http://www.westegg.com/bacon/
6. See the journal's website http://www.pubs.royalsoc.ac.uk/index.cfm?page=1085 where it is recorded 'The Royal Society was founded in 1660 to promote the new or experimental philosophy of that time, embodying the principles envisaged by Sir Francis Bacon. Henry Oldenburg was appointed as the first (joint) secretary to the Society and he was also the first editor of the Society's journal *Philosophical Transactions*'. The first issue appeared in 1665 and included Oldenburg's correspondence with some of Europe's scientists as well an account by Robert Boyle of a Very Odd Monstrous Calf. Subsequent early issues include 'articles' by Robert Hooke, Isaac Newton and Benjamin Franklin. The entire archive is available online.

7. See Sokal's webpage at http://www.physics.nyu.edu/faculty/sokal/. It includes the original paper published in *Social Text* and Sokal's explanation of why he wrote the article published in *Philosophy and Literature*. The Postmodernism Generator was written by Andrew C. Bulhak and modified slightly by Pope Dubious Provenance XI using the Dada Engine, a system for generating random text from recursive grammars.
8. See also the list of Collector's Items complied by Peter Krapp at http://www.hydra.umn.edu/derrida/coll.html

References

Bailey, C. W. Jr. (2001) Evolution of An Electronic Book: The scholarly electronic publishing bibliography, *The Journal of Electronic Publishing*, 7:2. Available at http://www.press.umich.edu/jep/07-02/bailey.html.

Bailey, C. W. Jr. (2006) *Scholarly Electronic Publishing Bibliography* (Houston, TX, Charles W. Bailey, Jr.) 1996–2006. Available at http://sepb.digital-scholarship.org/.

Berkenkotter, C. & Huckin, T. (1995) *Genre Knowledge in Disciplinary Communication: Cognition/culture power* (Hillsdale, NJ, Lawrence Erlbaum).

Bakhtin, M. (1986) *Speech Genres and Other Late Essays*, V. W. McGee, trans. (Austin, TX, University of Texas Press).

Bhatia, V. (2004) *Worlds of Written Discourse: A genre-based view* (London, Continuum).

Bolter, J. D. (1991) *Writing Space: The computer, hypertext, and the history of writing* (Hillsdale, NJ, Erlbaum).

Breure, L. (2001) Development of the Genre Concept. Available at http://people.cs.uu.nl/leen/GenreDev/GenreDevelopment.htm.

Canagarajah, S. (2002) *A Geopolitics of Academic Writing* (Pittsburgh, University of Pittsburgh Press).

Chandler, D. (n.d.) *Introduction to Genre Theory*. Available at http://www.aber.ac.uk/media/Documents/intgenre/intgenre.html.

Derrida, J. (1974) *Of Grammatology*, G. Chakravorty Spivak, trans. (Baltimore, MD, The Johns Hopkins University Press).

Derrida, J. (1980) The Law of Genre, *Critical Inquiry*, 7:1, pp. 55–72.

Derrida, J. (1983) The Time of a Thesis: Punctuations, K. McLaughlin, trans. in: A. Montefiore (ed.), *Philosophy in France Today* (Cambridge, Cambridge University Press), pp. 34–50.

Dutton, D. (1999) Language Crimes: A lesson in how not to write, courtesy of the professoriate, *The Wall Street Journal*, 5 February. Available at http://www.denisdutton.com/language_crimes.htm.

Ferris, S. P. (2002) Writing Electronically: The effects of computers on traditional writing, *The Journal of Electronic Publishing*, 8:1. Available at http://www.press.umich.edu/jep/08-01/ferris.html.

Fjällbrant, N. (1997) Scholarly Communication—Historical Development and New Possibilities, IATUL. Available at http://www.iatul.org/conference/proceedings/vol07/papers/full/nfpaper.html.

Kaufer, D. S. & Carley, K. M. (1993) *The Influence of Print on Sociocultural Organization And Change* (Hillsdale, NJ, LEA).

Lancashire, I. (2001) Lexicographical Meditations: A sense of genre. Available at http://lists.village.virginia.edu/lists_archive/Humanist/v14/0510.html.

Lang, B. (1983) *Philosophy and the Art of Writing: Studies in Philosophical and Literary Style* (Lewisburg, PA, Bucknell University Press; London, Associated University Presses).

Lavery, J. (2008) (ed.) *Literary Form, Philosophical Content: Historical studies in philosophical genre* (Madison, NJ, Fairleigh Dickinson University Press).

Marías, J. (1971; orig. 1953) Literary Genres in Philosophy, in: *Philosophy as Dramatic Theory*, J. Parsons, trans. (University Park, Pennsylvania State University Press), pp. 1–35.

Montaigne, M. (1575) Of the Education of Children, C. Cotton, trans. Available at http://oregonstate.edu/instruct/phl302/texts/montaigne/montaigne-essays-1.html#II.

Nentwich, M. (2003) *Cyberscience: Research in the age of the Internet* (Vienna, Austrian Academy of Sciences Press).

Nightingale, A. (1996) *Genres in Dialogue: Plato and the Construct of Philosophy* (Cambridge, Cambridge University Press).

Northrop Frye, H. (1957) *Anatomy of Criticism* (Princeton, NJ, Princeton University Press).

Rorty, R. (1982) Philosophy as a Kind of Writing: An essay on Derrida, in: R. Rorty (ed.), *Consequences of Pragmatism* (Brighton, Sussex, Harvester Press), pp. 90–109.

Russell, D. (2002) *Writing in the Academic Disciplines, 1870–1990: a curricular history* (Carbondale, IL, Southern Illinois University Press).

Valauskas, E. (1997) Waiting for Thomas Kuhn: First Monday and the evolution of electronic journals, *The Journal of Electronic Publishing*, 3:1. Available at http://www.press.umich.edu/jep/03-01/FirstMonday.html.

White, H. (2003) Anomalies of Genre: The utility of theory and history for the study of literary genres, *New Literary History*, 34:3, p. 597.

Woolgar, S. (ed.) (2000) *Virtual Society? Technology, cyberbole, reality* (Oxford, Oxford University Press).

2
Philosophical Writing: Prefacing as professing

Rob McCormack

Introduction

The following text documents the product of two years of compulsive writing and rewriting, work which was not so much intent on enacting a standard genre as it was a desperate effort to find/forge a range of appropriate and appropriable voices for writing a PhD, voices which whilst feeling 'real' to me could also meet the requirements of academic discourse It was only *after* this seemingly irrelevant work of 'prefacing' that I finally felt able to undertake the writing of the PhD itself. Much later—when the final thesis needed trimming—I was about to cut this entire Preface, when my supervisor intervened, insisting that 'it was the best part'! I was both shocked yet secretly pleased. To me there is a certain truth lodged in this Preface, even though—or perhaps—because it flouts the generic conventions of a standard preface. Certainly, it does grapple I believe with a liminal experience that is increasingly common, a profoundly cross-cultural, or rather cross-sectoral experience that is fraught with ambivalence, ambiguity and tension, an experience that I now observe in many other 'mature-aged' PhD students also returning to academe in order to reflect on their more 'worldly' life-worlds and domains of practice.

Actually, it was precisely this tension that shifted the ground of my thesis from applied linguistics and social theory into the clutches of philosophy. Only philosophy, it seemed, would allow the play of discourse voices necessary for exploring and articulating the issues I wished to explore, and yet as an academic discipline, philosophy, and as a genre, the PhD—both seemed to threaten this very play of voices.

Hence this extended Preface, grappling with questions of voice and genre, issues of 'ethos' and ethics, in an effort to find a 'pitch' (Cavell) that would discipline and support the writer whilst delimiting the strategies and expectations of the reader—all in the hope of beginning a fruitful conversation.

Preface[1]

A preface provides an author the opportunity to address the reader from the point of view of his authorship. Although etymologically a preface is a prefatory statement of the motivations and circumstances that surround the beginning of a project, there is a widespread practice of using the preface also to inform the reader about what is achieved in the end. A preface is thus at once a 'foreword' preceding the text and an 'afterword' following its completion; a curious combination of prologue and epilogue; a peculiar mix of promissory note and its redeemed cash value. Although a preface is placed first in the format, serialized by roman numerals so as to mark it off from the Arabic pagination of the main body of the text, it is written last. The writing of such a preface, binding beginning and end, becomes a burdensome task in the moment that the author becomes aware of the elusiveness of all beginnings and ends. Unable to surmount this elusiveness the author gravitates into a quandary as he deliberates on what is to be included and what is to be left out. (Scrag, 1989, p. vii)

A quarter of a century ago I purchased a book by an American philosopher whom I had earlier concluded was the only 'true' interpreter of Wittgenstein, the only commentator who 'really' understood Wittgenstein. This long-awaited text was a Harvard PhD thesis that had taken 20 years to reach publication. I learnt much later that it was probably the most photocopied PhD thesis in the history of analytic philosophy and had circulated widely in that format. Unfortunately I had not encountered any of these photocopies, and had been privy to only the vaguest of rumours concerning the significance of this unpublished work.

In excited anticipation I tore the wrapper open and began to read. Two pages later, I threw it down overwhelmed by anger and disgust. It would be many years before I revisited the writings of Stanley Cavell. And yet, time and again over recent years I have been drawn back to these very writings, always to the same uncanny ambivalence of repulsion and fascination.

The Rhetorical Tasks of Prefacing

According to Quintilian, who speaks from within the *sensus communis* of the theoretical and practical tradition of the 'art' of rhetoric:

> ... the sole purpose of the exordium is to prepare our audience in such a way that they will be disposed to lend a ready ear to the rest of our speech. The majority of authors agree that this is best effected in three ways, by making the audience well-disposed, attentive and ready to receive instruction. (Quintilian, *Inst*, IV.1.5)

Yet, the task of cultivating the good will and receptivity of an audience is especially difficult if one is intent on disrupting taken-for-granted protocols of listening and reading. In such a case the congeniality of the audience must be earned in face of an initial hostility and alienation, even 'anger and disgust'. Unfortunately, this thesis is intent on subverting the assumptions and conventions of the discourse of which it is part.

In this exordium or Preface I will work at distancing the tenor of this work from what, of course, in an institutional sense, it really is—a PhD thesis. As a genre, the

PhD is defined by its centrality to modern academic disciplines as 'Fächer', which posit themselves as cultivating disinterested and true bodies of knowledge representing their respective referential fields or domains of reality. Yet, this preface works hard at voiding, avoiding and evading this condition of its own existence. It works at throwing away the institutional ladder it has deployed in order to reach a perch from which to sing its song.

In fact, although I have headed this first Part of the thesis, 'Clearing the Ground', it may have been more apt to adduce a musical metaphor and to have titled it: 'Clearing the throat, finding a voice, establishing a key', because this thesis is endlessly prefaced by extensive preparations and prefacings heralding, deferring and displacing the actual moment of utterance. However, insofar as the task of this thesis is to teach a new and different mode of 'uptake', these prefacings are not simply neurotic or narcissistic efforts to forestall misunderstanding, but efforts to conjure a different ideal reader, to invite actual readers to take up a new stance towards the games of knowledge and truth.

The PhD and Practical Discourse

The reason for the obscurity and tortuousness of this Preface in accomplishing its work is that the shift from a modernist discourse of representation with its 'knowledge' and its 'objects of knowledge' to a practical discourse of articulation with its 'interpretations' of practical life and their convergences, is not easy to attain nor to maintain. Because the dominant discourse is the discourse of representation, it is easy, especially when writing within the generic constraints and affordances of the PhD genre, to lapse back into claims to superior knowledge; for the research PhD genre evolved precisely to enact this modernist discourse of knowledge, not the practical discourse of interpretation. Thus, for this thesis, the question of style is not just a matter of textual surface, of adding a dimension of rhetorical persuasion or aesthetic frisson to a self-same underlying prose of concepts.

Queering One's Discourse

To impale the reader on the issue of the differing genres within the prose of ideas and of which reading protocols we as readers adduce to our readings, I will adduce a lengthy and notorious passage from Stanley Cavell, the very passage that occasioned my anger and disgust, a passage which was Cavell's calculated effort at queering his discourse and thereby instructing his reader's reading of him away from a cognitivist reading and towards a more practical, perhaps even existential protocol of reading.

This Preface, however, also functions as an exorcism, as a frantic banging of lids and beating of drums, a cacophony intent on banishing once and for all the ghosts of 'representation' secreted within the pores of my own discourse, not just in the reading protocols of my reader. And yet I know that this is a forlorn hope: we cannot so easily evade the fact that we are constituted by what Gadamer terms 'the effects of actual history'. Just as we cannot make words mean whatever we like, so too we cannot control which realities or meanings are at play in our discourse and practice. I cannot predetermine the tenor or fate of this text simply by prefacing it with protestations of 'good intention' or by insisting on 'calling it (by my) names'. And yet I find myself compelled to attempt this very pre-determination.

That the discourse of modern knowledge and the PhD as a genre are mutually constitutive historical actualities is a fact, a fate. They encompass me, not me them. This I acknowledge: not with passive resignation, but as a historical reality and personal *habitus* to be continually re-worked, re-interpreted and resisted. In one sense the writing of this text is an extended Wittgensteinian therapeutic 'exercise' aimed at extirpating the metaphors of representation at work and at play within its author. This Preface is thus my impassioned (quixotic) attempt to forcibly, even violently, contribute to a re-figuring of both my own *habitus* and the conventions of the PhD as a genre by contributing to the emergence and legitimation of a different tenor in academic discourse, a tenor that is different from the 'normal' (Rorty) academic mode of address.

Ethics and Analysis

Recently I discovered that I was not alone in my response to the first two pages of Cavell's *The Claim of Reason*: apparently many readers had had the same reaction. We had all experienced this passage as a calculated assault. In those days, like most of Cavell's readers, I was a student of analytic philosophy possessed by a Cartesian dream of rigor, by its ruthless exploration of essence and its obsession with necessary and sufficient conditions.[2] Yet, even though I threw myself into this game of analysis with a passion, there was another reality to which I attributed even more seriousness— the domain of the ethical. This was a domain of such seriousness and personal significance that I refused to allow it to mix with academic discourse. There was the domain of the *fach*, of theory with its commitment to the rigor of the universal and impersonal concept; and there was the domain of ethics with its commitment to personal authenticity. These two regions were so at odds and so incommensurable that I refused to study any courses in ethics, aesthetics or politics at university. The thought of sitting in a tutorial with strangers debating ethical or political issues filled me with horror. Serious 'practical' discourse was for friends, not for anyone who happened to turn up to a tutorial. I therefore only read and wrote in the fields of general philosophy and philosophy of language.

As a further illustration of how deeply internalized the split in my life between the theoretical and the practical then, was: Towards the end of my schooling I decided that religion was a matter of personal conviction, not propositional knowledge. I concluded that it was immoral to learn the answers to religious questions: they should come from the heart or not at all. They certainly should not be rote learnt from the catechism the night before. I therefore refused to 'study' for Religious Instruction exams with dramatic effects: I plummeted from the top of the class to the bottom and was hauled before the principal of the school to be rebuked. It was, if you like, my first effort to confront the public world with the higher truth of 'the self', my first conscientious objection. (Cavell would see it as perhaps no accident that I was devouring *The Collected Works of Ralph Waldo Emerson* that year.)

Two Orders of Accountability

This clash between two orders of accountability was exacerbated by the culture of conviction cultivated by the student protest movement, the counter-culture and the New Left in the 1970s. Eventually I abandoned academic life. (For the record: the final straw was a shift in the paradigm from the analytical rigor of British Aristotelianism and Kantianism [think Ryle and Strawson] to the bizarre interweaving of logic, behaviourism and constructivist pragmatism of the Americans [think Quine]. In fact I found the prose and reasoning of Quine so arbitrary and strategic, that is, so pragmatic, that I realized the philosophical culture had changed into something in which I could no longer find myself.)

Clearly, my habitation with these competing orders—an order of the objective and an order of the subjective, the domain of persons as end in themselves and the domain of persons as institutional instruments and roles, between culture and society, between the private world of creativity and freedom centred on 'the work of art', and the public world of 'the system' of convention, rules, obligation, norms, regulation, and law—was not a personal psychic idiosyncrasy, but my inhabiting of the social order of liberalism itself. This *habitus* was intensified by a schooling that created a 'doubled subject'. As someone being initiated into literate modes of colonial and cosmopolitan forms of life far beyond the ken of my immediate family and community, and as a boy in a boarding school conducted according to the disciplinary (Foucault), the sense of an alienation between the charged and meaningful world of the individual on the one hand and the mundane, arbitrary accommodations of institutions on the other, was absolutely palpable to me. Crudely: the only place you could be free was to invent a personal world in your own head and inhabit it. These worlds were to be found in the worlds of books. By entering the world of books you could escape the determinations of place and time anchored to the institutional body.

Reprise

Twenty-five years later I find myself still worrying at these same issues, but now Cavell's prose looks differently to me. Now that I too am trying to knead my thoughts into the protean generic constraints of a PhD, I find myself 'understanding' what Cavell was worrying at all that time ago. Wittgenstein once said of his own work that his writings were probably only understandable by someone who had already had similar thoughts. Let's take 'similar thoughts' to mean 'similar worries' and say: I now understand Cavell better because or insofar as I now share what he was worried about back then.

So, what are these worries that Cavell had back then and that I now also experience? They are issues to do with mode of address in philosophical discourse. They are issues such as: is philosophical discourse merely academic discourse, the discourse of a *Fach*, or is it something different? And if (like Cavell or myself) you don't wish to construe philosophical discourse as simply a discourse of cognition, a theoretical discourse—if you believe that it is also a practical discourse, a discourse of ethics, of politics, of responsibility, of living, a discourse that is claimed by and projects a claim that is 'more than' the expression of a doctrine or theory within a discipline within the academic division of labour that is the modern university—how should you write? How should you present yourself? How should you frame the authority of your discourse? In short, *who do you think you are?* And *what do you think you are doing?*

Cavell's Opening Passage

So, let's look back to that passage that was so offensive to me along with so many others—the first two paragraphs of Cavell's *The Claim of Reason*:

> If not at the beginning of Wittgenstein's late philosophy, since what starts philosophy is no more to be known at the outset than how to make an end to it; and if not at the opening of *Philosophical Investigations*, since its opening is not to be confused with the starting of the philosophy it expresses, and since the terms in which that opening might be understood can hardly be given along with the opening itself; and if we acknowledge from the commencement, anyway leave open at the opening, that the way this work is written is internal to what it teaches, which means that we cannot understand the manner (call it method) before we understand its work: and if we do not look to our history, since placing this book historically can hardly happen earlier than placing it philosophically; nor look to Wittgenstein's past, since then we are likely to suppose that the *Investigations* is written in criticism of the *Tractatus*, which is not so much wrong as empty, both because to know what constitutes its criticism would be to know what constitutes its philosophy, and because it is more to the present point to see how the *Investigations* is written in criticism of itself: then where and how are we to approach this text? How shall we let this book teach us, this or anything?
>
> I will say first, by way of introducing myself and saying why I insist, as I will throughout the following pages, upon the *Investigations* as a philosophical text, that I have wished to understand philosophy not as a set of problems but as a set of texts. This means to me that the contribution of a philosopher—anyway of a creative thinker—to the subject of philosophy is not to be understood as a contribution to, or of, a set of *given* problems, although both historians and non-historians of the subject are given to suppose otherwise.—And is the remark about texts and not problems itself to be taken as a philosophical text? It seems argumentative or empty enough, since obviously not all texts are philosophical ones, but only those that precisely contain problems of a certain sort!—The fact that the remark is short would be no bar to that status. Many philosophical texts are short, like the tattle tale told by a Cretan, or the story about the tree falling in the forest for no one to hear. Some philosophers are able to make about anything into a philosophical text, like a preacher improving upon the infant's first cry; while some

people are not even able to start a quarrel with God. Some texts are as long as long books, but generally treated as though they are sets of given problems, something between conundrums and formal arguments, e.g. Hume's *Treatise*, which few seem actually to believe but which many feel compelled to try to outsmart; as if so *much* argument just oughtn't to stand unanswered; as if to contribute a text were a kind of defacement; as if argumentative victory *consisted* in spoils. Some philosophical texts are as short as short books, e.g. Descartes' *Meditations*, which so refines our essential options for philosophical belief that thinkers have seemed, since its appearance, and whether invited or not, compelled to reply to it; as if so *little* argument just oughtn't to stand unanswered. When its conclusions have seemed more or less disreputable its repliers have focussed on its 'methods', hoping to head the conclusions off, or outnumber them. But I think one feels the knack of the methods (call it the arrogance) to be missed, which is no doubt something that perpetuates fascination with this text; as though its repliers find it incredible that one could, truly and legitimately *use oneself* (clearly and distinctly) in arriving at conclusions so strange and so familiar. But in philosophy to find that position incredible may well amount to disbelieving that one could oneself contribute a philosophical text. Some philosophical texts are for practical purposes as unending as the writing of, for example Kant or Hegel, where the problem resides largely in mastering the text itself, hence in commentary; as though if one could believe *all* of it there would from then on be no isolating problems of belief left. (So Kierkegaard condemned the system; so Nietzsche condemned it). Here contribution consists in opting to be marginal (which is of course not the only way of *being* marginal.) (You may think of these instances as beginning a budget of philosophical genres or paradigms. Then someone will think that I have been arrogantly neglectful of the genre of the academic paper, modest in its aims, content with its minor addition to a subject greater than itself. About the comparative greatness of the subject over its subjects I have no doubt. But I would be more than convinced of academic modesty had I not seen many who are daily surprised that, for example, Descartes or Pascal or Rousseau, or the spirit of religion or of rationalism or of romanticism, has survived the criticism fashioned in their essays on the subjects a few years back. I speak of professional lives, frightening matters.) (Cavell, 1979, pp. 3–5)

As you can imagine (if you survived the reading of it), this opening is deliberately crafted as a provocation to the tradition of analytic philosophy, which at the time was smugly ensconced in English-speaking universities. It provoked the predictable response. 'Anyone writing like this is obviously a poseur, an amateur, someone displaced from a literature department; they are clearly not a philosopher within the modern progressive discipline of philosophy.[3] If this is meant to be serious academic writing, where is the overview? Where are the Topic Sentences? Does this Professor of Philosophy from Harvard really know what he is talking about?'

Provocation, not Propositions

At first blush, such a mode of writing is outrageous—it is common knowledge that that first sentence consists of two hundred and sixteen words—yet on closer examination it is absolutely faithful to its own understanding of what a philosophical text is. If we glance back to the dedication page of *The Claim of Reason*, we find a citation from Ralph Waldo Emerson:

> Truly speaking, it is not instruction, but provocation, that I can receive from another soul.

'Provocation' not 'instruction': a discourse that does not so much try to tell the reader what to think, but one that *makes them think*, provokes them into thinking (their own thoughts). Dialogue: not as agreement or consensus but as mutual provocation. Discourse: not as excavating the same ontology but as provoking the reader into grasping their own subjectivity, their own responsibility, their own world. Obviously we have here a mode of address from the same family (of philosophical genres) as Socrates' dialectic or Kierkegaard's mode of indirect address, a form of address intent on provoking subjectivity rather than imposing system or dogma.

Generic Constraints

I have often wondered at my 'cruelty' in subjecting the reader to this long and torturous passage from Cavell. This insistence I initially experienced more as a compulsion than as a rational or justified choice. My feelings fluctuated widely and wildly: sometimes taking the form of resentment ('Take that, you academically ensconced PhD marker!'). Even so, I felt that citing the passage was not merely a matter of personal feeling or private revenge. My reluctance to cut the quote was vindicated by a recent reading of Amelie Oksenberg Rorty's 'Experiments in Philosophic Genre: Descartes' *Meditations*' (Rorty, 1983). In this article Rorty explores the contrast between philosophy as a 'precision of argument' and philosophy as a 'rhetoric of persuasion'. She marks a distinction between academic philosophy written 'like scientific writing ... in the "article" mode' and 'those of us who realize that any serious philosophic enterprise is, whether we like it or not, implicitly a moralizing one'. But these latter (which includes of course Cavell and myself):

> ... place ourselves in a delicate and ambiguous position. Though normally addicted to self-referential issues, we philosophers have avoided openly discussing our own problems of style and genre, taking evasive action to assure respectability by following pervasive fashions. And not without reason: To whom can we speak about the difficulties of stylistic choice, and in what voice. (Rorty, 1983, p. 547)

Need I say that Cavell's opening paragraphs precisely are intended to plunge the (philosophical) reader directly and inescapably into the question of genre, style and voice. And I have adduced *his* beginning as *my* beginning to also openly foreground these issues of style, voice and address, rather than evade them in the interests of respectability.

The Ancient Genre of Meditation

Rorty interprets Descartes' *Meditations* as an appropriation of traditional meditation genres. She notes how Descartes re-works the genre in order to substitute an intellectual transformation for the older Stoic transformation of the self. But what interests me at this juncture is that there is a common narrative movement in meditations as a genre, whether they be what Rorty terms 'ascensional' or 'penitential'. Ascensional mediations draw on neo-Platonic metaphors regarding light and illumination and the gradual clarification of a mind that has 'forgotten' what it somehow already knows. Penitential meditations, by contrast, construe the reader as not merely confused or uncentred, but as 'fallen', as 'perverse'. Such a condition calls for more radical provocations on the part of the writer. 'When the reader-penitent is unaware of his fallen condition, he must first be brought to a state of despair'.

It is with this insight that I now understand my compulsion to include such a cruel quotation. Rather than simply an exercise in resentment, my use of this quote is a move in a traditional philosophic genre. It was this compulsion I was subject to. The quotation is intended to bring the reader to 'a state of despair'. It is the modern counterpart to ancient *ascepsis* as an essential hinge in the transformation of the self through philosophic practice (Hadot, 1995).

Two Forms of Penitential Meditation

However, Rorty addresses something further that is pertinent to the endless prefacing enacted in this thesis. She writes:

> [T]here are two versions of the penitential meditation. In the first, all the stages leading to the true self are transcended, the ladder is kicked away at the end. The new person bears no continuous relation to the old, not even to the self who undertook the penitential quest: everything about the past self, even his motives for seeking the Way, is suspect and must be abandoned. Even when such a penitential meditation is intellectual rather than passionate or spiritual, skeptical cleansing is only provisional. Once truth has been found, and skepticism reveals itself as self-destructive, skepticism can be abandoned. But in the second version of the penitential mode, all the stages of the penitential quest are continuously preserved, continuously reenacted. Even the mediating skeptical ascepsis, the cleansing of error, is always still required, even after the self is transformed, fully realized. (Rorty, 1983, p. 552)

The inability of the second mode of penitential meditation to throw away the ladder of epistemological scepticism and to get on with the task of picturing the true, perfectly captures my own compulsion to keep the question of textuality alive, my inability to pass beyond it to the 'self-certifying criterion' of modern philosophical discourse. It also accounts for my ambivalent nods in the direction of Derrida. Clearly he is lodged inextricably in this second version of penitential meditation:

he spends his entire effort demonstrating that we cannot step off the ladder onto stable or common ground. We are forever 'in process', climbing the ladder of sceptical *différance*, never to arrive. Again, what can I say? I recognize myself hovering (stranded?) between these two versions, or uses, of scepticism: one, as a preliminary purging phase in a larger movement of thought; the second, as an unavoidable condition inf(l)ecting all human thought (and action).

The Language of Cavell

Now for some comments on the language of this passage from Cavell. Surely you could not have missed all the appositives (the 'as if's); all the bracketed asides and Cavell's own strange use of the dash at the beginnings of sentences; the sheer length of some of the sentences and the shortness of others; and the systematic ambiguity of the deictic in phrases such as 'this work', 'this book': is it our reading of Cavell or Cavell's reading of Wittgenstein? and so on. Here, we have a prose that straddles the boundary between philosophy and literature, between a discourse of reason and a discourse of life, between the grammar of writing and the grammar of speech. In writing of this order the difference between a reality existing prior to the writing (writing as *Nachbild*) and a reality being enacted (produced, provoked) by the writing itself (writing as *Vorbild*) seems to blur.

Notice also the liberal deployment of 'I'. There is nothing impersonal, no offer of a universal subject position for the reader to assume or take up here. Rather, the self of the text seems deliberately 'provocative' and challenging. Clearly, Cavell is insisting that we are not going to come away from reading his text with any 'clear and distinct' propositions or professional concepts. Right at the beginning he is giving us a reading lesson about how, or rather how not, to read his work. This reading lesson is not a matter of communicating facts about the reading process, nor a matter of specifying a theory of reading, but more a matter of forcing a mode of reading on us by blocking our familiar strategies of reading such as looking for the concepts or the causal relationships between the facts. Cavell disables our normal modern modes of reading, let's call it factual or cognitivist reading. It was this that provoked my refusal to continue reading twenty five years ago.

How to Read

Instead of expounding or justifying a theory of reading he thematizes the very issue of 'how to approach or begin reading a book' by talking about how to read Wittgenstein's *Philosophical Investigations*. But of course this is allegory, an indirect way of instructing us how to read his own book, *The Claim of Reason*. In both cases, 'the way this work is written is internal to what it teaches, which means that we cannot understand the manner (call it method) before we understand its work'. In other words, both texts are intent on teaching new modes of discourse, new ways of reading and writing, and thus new ways of being (who we are) by recalling (re-collecting, re-finding, remembering, reaffirming, rearticulating, revisioning, revising) what matters most to us (the contours of the world we live in). Both want to teach us, want us to learn, 'how to be' as much as 'how things are'. Both want to teach us that 'how things are' is a matter of 'how we are'. The world disclosed to us is internally related to our mode of Being-in-the-world, and this is not a matter of Consciousness. These matters are not amenable to straightforward deliberation or will power. We cannot change our modes of reading and writing just be trying. We have to be drawn, seduced, provoked, into the play of these reflective modes of literacy, usually by a teacher or writer.

But notice the careful staging of all this. The first paragraph does not have a single 'I' in it. It is all 'we', 'we', 'we':

> If not at the beginning of Wittgenstein's late philosophy, since what starts philosophy is no more to be known at the outset than how to make an end to it; and if not at the opening of *Philosophical Investigations*, since its opening is not to be confused with the starting of the philosophy it expresses, and since the terms in which that opening might be understood can hardly be given along with the opening itself; and if **we** acknowledge from the commencement, anyway leave open at the opening, that the way this work is written is internal to what it teaches, which means that **we** cannot understand the manner (call it method) before we understand its work: and if **we** do not look to our history, since placing this book historically can hardly happen earlier than placing it philosophically; nor look to Wittgenstein's past, since then **we** are likely to suppose that the *Investigations* is written in criticism of the *Tractatus*, which is not so much wrong as empty, both because to know what constitutes its criticism would be to know what constitutes its philosophy, and because it is more to the present point to see how the *Investigations* is written in criticism of itself: then where and how are **we** to approach this text? How shall **we** let this book teach **us**, this or anything? (Cavell, 1979, my bolding)

We are seduced into a community of consensus, although we also feel as if we are being spun around too fast and getting dizzy. We suspect we are being bullied. Suddenly, in the second paragraph, Cavell dramatically shifts footing and takes up a new subject position: he backs off from speaking on our behalf, on behalf of a community and institutes a distance between himself and the community in general. He becomes an 'I'.

Community and Responsibility

Yet notice the irony in the way he uses 'I' four times to 'take shots' at academic discourse:

> About the comparative greatness of the subject over its subjects **I** have no doubt. But **I** would be more than convinced of academic modesty had **I** not seen many who are daily surprised that, for example, Descartes or Pascal or Rousseau, or the spirit of religion or of rationalism or of romanticism, has survived the criticism fashioned in their essays on the

subjects a few years back. **I** speak of professional lives, frightening matters. (Cavell, 1979, my bolding)

Again, provocation! In the very act of insisting that the community of philosophy is prior to the individual philosopher, even to Wittgenstein, he uses the first person! He could have written:

Undoubtedly a subject is greater than its subjects.

Instead he writes:

About the comparative greatness of the subject over its subjects **I have no doubt** (my bolding).

Using Halliday's (1985) linguistic categories, it is clear that the normal unmarked word order of this sentence has been reversed to place the 'I have no doubt' in the NEW position at the end of the sentence. The focus of the sentence is thus on *his* assessment, *his* judgement, *his* playing 'critical subject' over against the impersonal and anonymous *Fach* of philosophy. What the one hand gives, the other takes back! In the act of acknowledging the priority and authority of the discipline (objectivity, the universal), he simultaneously makes it clear that it is he, *Cavell*, who is saying this; it is he, *Cavell*, who makes this judgment. He is playing with us! What does he really think? He is toying with us! What do we think? He is just being provocative! But: is it or isn't it? Is the community of philosophical discourse prior to its subjects or not? What do you think? What do *you* think?—Gotcha! This is a prose intent on provoking its reader into thought, not just in the sense of entering into a discourse community but even more in the sense of taking up a new stance towards oneself and one's ways of discoursing. It is a prose of discomfort, a prose that sets out to disturb and disrupt 'where you're at', rather than seduce (persuade, reason) you seamlessly into a new view.

Disciplining the Reader

Notice that this form of address clearly transgresses both disciplinary boundaries and the border between academic discourse and non-academic discourse. Whether students (such as myself) can deploy such a prose or discourse—a post-epistemological form of discourse, a discourse that disrupts the pretensions of cognitivist discourse and its claims to expertise, a discourse that is at once provocative yet reasoning, playful yet responsible, a discourse that listens to the other in the self and the self in the other—in their PhDs (outside literature departments) without being failed, is problematic. Notice how difficult it is to read the grammar of some of these sentences—most of Cavell's and some of mine—like that last one. Notice how the passage is sprinkled with commands: 'Call it method'; 'Call it arrogance'; 'Notice ...'. Again, these are highly involving and dialogic. They are ways of provoking, not just persuading. (Notice that three sentences in this paragraph—four if we include this one as well—are imperatives, commands, beginning with 'Notice'.) What sort of method is this sort of telling, a telling that uses commands instead of description and reason? What sort of discipline is such an overt discipline?

Writing and Institution

Notice how (but also notice how you noticed the 'Notice ...' this time) Cavell's writing is a writing that moves to the rhythms of speech. Its grammar is as sinuous, as subtle and as extended as the grammar of speech (as analyzed by Halliday, 1987). It is a writing that seems not to care about its overall (global, generic) shape, a prose that simply follows the logic of the local, that moves forward by injecting a new spin on the preceding thought. There seems to be no clear linear direction nor transparent hierarchy of principles or levels. The clauses seem to tumble over one another, interrupt one another, compete with one another.

It is as if this writing is no longer answerable to an institutional setting or the constraints codified in the structures of academic genres. It is as if it has escaped from the ordinary institutional imperatives of academic discourse. There is no clear demarcation between language and meta-language, between the world of objects and the interpretations of those objects, between things and discourse. The order of things and the order of discourse are construed as mutually constitutive. There is no clear distinction between the order of concepts and the order of facts, between the order of principles and the order of instances, between the order of universals and the order of particulars, between the order of ideas and the order of examples, between the order of meanings and the order of events, between the order of reality and the order of discourse, between the order of assertion and the order of commentary, between the order of discourse and the order of meta-discourse, between the order of content and the order of logic, or between essence and form.

Philosophy as a Kind of Writing

Whereas cognitivist writing is strictly organized in terms of 'relationships of content'—Halliday's (1985) external conjunction—, and adversarial writing is organized in terms of 'reasons for saying'—Halliday's (1985) internal conjunction—, this mode of writing (whose? Wittgenstein's? Cavell's? mine?) is looser. It is a discourse that constructs its present and future as growing reflectively out of its past. It is a discourse that does not so much try to discover the new as re-appropriate the past as a resource for making meaning in the present. It does not move on to new topics as an opening up of new worlds but as new ways of making meaning out of its own resources, new ways of weaving the resources of its existing habitat and *habitus*. The emphasis is on adjusting and reworking earlier meanings whether they are the meanings of ego or meanings of alter. The focus is on trying to unpack, to clarify, to articulate, to reactivate, to re-gloss communal meanings. There is no claim to finality or mastery, but rather a claim to awakening which is at the same time a claim to participation. Cavell himself constantly problematizes and thematizes his own prose and its mode of address. He is textually self-conscious. For Cavell philosophy is a mode of address. For Cavell philosophy is a mode of address that turns you, tropes you, that makes you think. Philosophy is a kind of writing, a writing that disrupts the normalizing communicative dimension of language as communicating a taken-for-granted content, grammar, or world. Philosophy wants to disrupt, defamiliarize that world.

Philosophy as Ergon

If philosophy is discourse, a work, that works on the reader, puts the reader to work, makes the reader work, then it cannot aspire to the modern notion of prose as the transparent communication (of facts, concepts or ideas). In a recent text, Cavell has himself thematized the mode of address of philosophical texts under the headings of 'sociability' and 'geniality' in order to open up the possibility of a writer wishing to queer their text and refuse to communicate:

> My use of 'sociality' is meant to problematize the idea of a work's 'audience', to suggest that, perhaps most definitively for romantic writing, the quest for audience is exactly as questionable as that for expression: it is no *given* set (assembly, class) of hearers or readers that is sought, or fantasized. 'Geniality' I mean to problematize the idea of a work's 'intention', or an author's taking of the reader into his or her confidence: author and reader will be like-minded if they are congeners, generated together, of one another ... . A further region of 'sociality' and 'geniality' invites (unlike 'audience' or 'intention') the issue of a text's unsociability or ungeniality, its power to repel, its unapproachability marked as its reproachfulness. (Cavell, 1979, p. 12)

Now we can begin to 'get a bead on' what Cavell is 'up to' in those first two paragraphs of *The Claim of Reason*: he is deliberately repelling, resisting, disarming, disabling a certain mode of reading, reproaching those who construe the reading and writing of philosophy that way; resisting, denying, declining, evading that sort of discourse, that sort of philosophy, that sort of thinking, that sort of life, that way of being with your self, with your life and with others, of living in that sort of world, of being that sort of person. Those like myself who were unthinkingly immersed in that life and world, the world of academic philosophy, felt baffled, hurt, rejected, angry.

Policing the Subject

But: is this mode of writing riding for a fall? Is it deluding itself? Is it dependent on the very institutional conditions it pretends to evade? Is Bourdieu right in insisting that:

> In the beginning is the *illusio*, adherence to the game, the belief of whoever is caught in the game, the interest for the game, interest *in* the game, the founding of value, *investment* in both the economic and psychoanalytic sense. The institution is inseparable from the founding of the game, which as such is arbitrary, and from the constitution of the disposition to be taken in by the game, whereby we lose sight of the

arbitrariness of its founding and, in the same stroke, recognize the necessity of the institution. *Esse est interesse*: Being is being in, it is belonging and being possessed, in short participating, taking part, according importance, interest. (Bourdieu, 1983, p. 1)

Can you write like Cavell only when you are (already) a professor at Harvard? Bourdieu, Fish (1990) and Hunter all construe this sort of prose as misrecognising its embeddedness within the *Fach* of modern academic philosophy which is in turn located within that cognitive division of labour which is the modern university. I disagree; and this thesis will follow Gadamer in retrieving an older mode of discourse—practical philosophy—that underpins the disciplines of social science, the humanities and the arts, and even all social discourse and action. The Gadamerian claim for the universality of hermeneutics is at once a claim for the universality of practical philosophy and *phronesis*.

Terrain and Map

I too have been evading a mode of address that conforms with the requirements of an academic *Fach*, a prose ordered by the logical development of a central line of argument within a stable disciplinary frame. I find myself repeatedly setting off down favoured discursive paths. Yet despite my persistence, these paths will not form themselves into a linear route or highway. I feel like Wittgenstein's philosopher who comes to know a forest by continually venturing into it but always by a different path. When you do this, you develop a feel or sense of a terrain, but a sense that is below the threshold of analytic or logical articulation. It is as if knowledge of the territory is a familiarity founded on longevity and intimacy of use, not formal training into analytic modes of representation and discourse.

And, in my case, this is in fact true: I am indeed writing about matters I have not been formally or academically trained into, but they are topics I find myself compelled to revisit over and over for practical nourishment, refreshment and guidance. On these visits I typically read the textual terrain of philosophy by allowing myself to be drawn from one passage or phrasing to another as if my attention or eye is being drawn by the brightness of a flower here or the grandness of a tree root there. A reading of ex-stasis; a reading of submission, a flowing with the text. A reading in search of what?—the flash of a metaphor or phrase. Elbow's (1981) believing game; Gadamer's *Spiel* (1989). Definitely not the detached distance of the spectator or the academic carefully and consciously noting and discursively formulating their field notes.

Reading as Practical Reflection

Reading as spiritual sustenance; reading as a gentle submission to the 'forceless force of ideas' (Habermas). Reading as the nurturing of a *Sache* (Gadamer); reading as trying to gradually find that you have forged 'natural' connections between disparate regions of meaning. Reading as the gentle interleaving of disparate discourses in mutually illuminating ways, ways that do not violently impose one on the other as meta- or master discourse, a weaving that seems to arise from and 'present' (*darstellen*) a constellation or force field, a common ground that is not purely personal nor merely conceptual, a common ground, that is *there* (*Dasein*) in our practices, a common ground that (now that we can sense it, perhaps even formulate it) allows our practices to be more themselves. Thus, a reading that is both a finding and a forging, a reading that is both a discovery and a fashioning, a reading that discloses the lifeworld of our practices and thereby enables us to reinvent these practices. Reading as reflection on *praxis*, as thinking towards *praxis*, thinking over *praxis*, thinking back across *praxis*, thinking as *nachdenken*. Thinking as reminiscence, as re-visioning, as revising, as going back over what has happened and what was said, re-encountering the contours, the terrain of possibilities and possible paths, the pervading otherness and absence inhabiting the event, its other possibilities and potentialities, its constraints and affordances, its dead-ends and its growth points. Reading as professional meditation, as ethical recollection. But not: reading as academic discourse.

The effect of such modes of reading is that ideas, as it were, can 'well up'; they are 'ready to hand'; part of a *habitus*: part of a life-world. I can speak fragments of coherent abstract discourse. Having immersed myself in a *copia* of philosophical discourse, I do not run dry of ideas. In this sense I am like a Renaissance rhetorician. But, like all Renaissance men of letters, I lack method, system or logic. My discourse is governed by an assemblage of commonplace *topoi* and tropes that 'get me by', that do the job, that allow me 'to go on' (Wittgenstein), that keep the conversation going (Rorty, 1980). Bacon, Descartes and Ramus would, rightly, dis(ap)prove its lack of rigor and clarity, its placid accommodation to the exigencies and contours of terrain and audience, its avoidance of the hard questions, its evasion of the duty to bulldoze these paths and their horizons into a single deductive highway built on unshakable foundations. In short, its refusal, or evasion, of the canons of modernity.

Practical Philosophy

Instead of Habermas' 'philosophy with a practical intent', I am suggesting a '*praxis* with philosophical intent'. Whereas Habermas imagines the relations between philosophy and *praxis* through the Kantian metaphor of the relation between the *a priori* and the empirical, in which the Kantian *a priori* determines either constitutively or regulatively, I am returning to the traditional Aristotelian sense of practical philosophy as a cultivation of the *sensus communis*, as a conversation that discloses what is common, what is between us, in which we see ourselves as forming a community of practice and speech. We don't bring philosophy or theory to *praxis*. Rather, in our practicing we find ourselves reaching for theory to make sense of our practice, a *praxis* that always outreaches ourselves and our understanding, that is in its most important moments always other than us.

Later, I will adduce Gadamer's insistence that our insertion in practice (or discourse or life) is more like being thrown into and caught up in a game, a game that is not of our own choosing or making, a game in which we do not know or decide the rules but in which we can only make our moves and try to change the rules as responses to what happens, a game in which we cannot go back and start again,[4] thus a historical game constituted by events and effects that cannot be undone or reversed. I find this a more fruitful image of *praxis* and the driven-ness of our reaching for theory or philosophy as a way of trying to make sense of what we are caught up in.

Theory

But this image also makes clear why we are continually tempted by a theoreticist or cognitivist notion of theory, by a theory offering to reach beyond our situatedness and institute order and discipline for *praxis*. Hence the Kantian project of modernity. Theory as concepts for ordering (putting in order, giving orders). Theory as 'boss man'. Theory as telling practitioners what we really can or should be, what things are (called), how we should experience things, how things are, who we are, and what we are doing. Theory as legislator. Theory as ruler. Theory as 'the Subject'. Theory as and for 'the State'.

This Kantian rendering of theory will be an important locus around which this thesis will circle. It will feature as a marker, a horizon, a project signifying an inescapable temptation within practice. I will be arguing that it is precisely this modernist Kantian account of reason that must be deconstructed and replaced with a more modest, more localized and more 'in process' rendering of reason as a measure of the value or truth of practices and discourse. This Kantian moment of legislation is akin to the Gorgian moment in Plato in which Socrates demarcates between the selfless purity of his own truth-seeking philosophical discourse compared with the interested, manipulative rhetorical discourse of Gorgias. Both constitute attacks on the finitude of vernacular practices, understandings and discourses. Both posit a purer domain of reality which can be used as 'measures of accountability' in order to bring reason, order and clarity to the disorder, ambiguity and obscurity of customary ways which subsist as ontological social practices, as sensibilities and *habitus*.

Will's (1988) development of the concept of governance so that it is not confined to what he calls 'deductive governance', which is narrowly focussed on abstract written or symbolic representations of norms and practices is helpful at this point. Will supplements the rationalism and textualism of this deductive governance with a more contextual reflexivity situated at the moment of application or use, which he calls 'ampliative governance'. Although he uses the phrase 'governance of norms', Will insists that it is imperative not to confuse what he calls 'norms' with their textual or symbolic representations. His use of the term 'norm' is intended to embody the same range and 'thickness' as such terms as 'rule' in Wittgenstein's language games, 'internal good' in MacIntyre's 'practices', 'custom' in Hegel, or '*habitus*' in Bourdieu. Will also adduces Dewey's treatment of 'habit' (including custom) in *Human Nature and Conduct* (1922) and Kuhn's (1970) notion of 'paradigms' as terms of a comparable order. So, even though a 'norm' is what serves as a guide or standard of thought and action, Will is concerned to demonstrate that norms are practical human realities that cannot be reduced to their textual, linguistic or symbolic representations, and that the governance of norms as a practice extends deep into everyday *praxis*, far beyond the self-conscious and explicitly deliberative discourse of the Kantian tribunal of 'reason' in which norms are subjected to even more abstract norms.

Philosophy is Unforgettable

Although philosophy may repudiate rhetoric and opinion (*endoxa*) as untruth, this act of rejection is itself an act that is never finalized but instead one of eternal vigilance (and I would suggest perversely that this vigil is now maintained by that wide-awake reader, Derrida). The true philosopher in modernity is the philosopher who attends to this Gorgian moment revealing it as a moment that cannot be completed, a ladder that cannot be thrown away. Philosophy is condemned to discursively articulate itself as both rhetoric and language. But for all this, Derrida does not repudiate philosophy itself, as Foucault and some of his followers have tried: Derrida is not a positivist. We will 'forget Foucault' long before we 'forget philosophy'. But of course even Foucault could not forget philosophy, no matter how far he fled. 'Final Foucault' is in fact Foucault's coming home to philosophy, to philosophy as a practice of liberty. We can never be *after logos*. We can never rid ourselves of the aspirations of philosophy, but nor can they be directly enacted as both Plato and Kant seemed to have suggested. I write 'seemed' because later we will note Gadamer's claim that there is another Plato besides this metaphysical Plato. There is also Plato the author of dialogues that in their very form undercut claims to metaphysical truth. Similarly, some commentators interpret Kant's third critique, *Critique of Judgment*, as his belated attempt to formulate a bridge to mediate between the world of the transcendental and the world of the empirical that were so severely and emphatically separated in his two earlier critiques.

Practical Philosophy: Back to the Rough Ground

The point is to deconstruct the binarisms of metaphysics, not to occupy either pole; to refuse universalizing theory, but also to refuse the monadic intuitions of situated particularity—to mobilize a different 'mixture' of truth-telling; to enact a voice that is neither solely prophetic, solely scientific, solely bureaucratic, solely procedural, or solely reflective, a voice that reworks all of these into a more practical moment; a voice that attempts to be commensurate and responsibly worldly, without abandoning a horizon of values; a voice that is commensurate with Wittgenstein's observation on the desire for transcendence:

> … we have got onto slippery ice where there is no friction and so in a certain sense the conditions are ideal, but also, just because of that, we are unable to walk. We want to walk: so we need *friction*. Back to the rough ground! (Wittgenstein, 1963, para. 107)

Practical philosophy is the discipline whose historical charter is the cultivation of this rough ground, the terrain on which the written texts of legislators intersect with the reflective interpretations arising out of the situated *habitus* of practitioners. My hope is to produce a text that walks by depicting literacy practices that walk; I am too old to dream of flying any more. But surely we can walk with dignity, justice, solidarity and virtue. Walking does not only have value or meaning as the fore-runner, beginning of, precursor for, or fallen substitute for—running ... or flying.

Mundane Transcendence: Praxis or the State

Ian Hunter (1994) would insist that my text (or practice) is 'unwarranted' because these different forms of truth-telling are located within different and incommensurable 'departments of life'. Hunter, like Fish, is a high modernist, not as might at first seem, a postmodernist. Both deploy sceptical arguments to erect high boundaries between the different institutional domains of contemporary social life. The difference is that Hunter allows a mundane universal governance to 'governmentality'. Hunter's boundaries are penetrable from the side of governmentality—but not from the side of critique or cultivation. For Hunter, the State seems to occupy a worldly horizon of transcendence, if we could put it in such a paradoxical way. Certainly for Hunter, the State is not simply yet another local region of practices or institutions; it occupies a privileged position. Why? Well, not because of a originary 'social contract', nor does it seem to be because it possesses an empirical monopoly on power and violence.

Committed to assigning a historically contingent and conjunctural existence to 'the State', what can Hunter possibly say about why it possesses this privileged position, about why it should be obeyed, about why it should be able to decide education policy. In fact, what we find at this point in Hunter is a peculiar ambivalence regarding the status and authority of 'governmentality'. On the one hand, he insists its emergence is a historically contingent event occasioned by the religious wars of the seventeenth century and that an understanding emerged to institute a new form of the State that did not implicate transcendental or religious values or forms of reasoning. It was a State committed to the mundane values of life. Notice that this is not the 'neutral state of liberalism' which rejects all notions of the good, but the police state, a state committed to the value of wealth, prosperity, peace and security.

The Paradox of Boundaries

But now comes the paradox: why should we be bound by this historically contingent form of the State? Hunter might reply: because, empirically, these are our practices. But he wants to go further and say: because we can't think outside this form; because we can't be different; and, even on occasion, because we *shouldn't* think or act outside this form or constellation of practices and discourses. Now, there is always a problem with setting limits. Every child knows that a limit institutes a temptation to put your toe across the line. 'You can't think that!' 'Can't think what?' 'You can't think that critics engaged in self-cultivation should be allowed or able to criticize policies and practices of the bureau'. 'Right! Thanks for spelling out what is not thinkable. It obviously is thinkable and does make sense. So, you must really be saying: Don't (you shouldn't) think it.'

Hunter knows that transcendental arguments don't work. So, why try to hold us to some 'understanding' or 'agreement' about how to interpret the State. Of course, Hunter wants to say: 'Because they are simply and empirically the practices we have, and to attempt to leap beyond them is dangerous'. But my reply is that we are not confined to our present practices: we possess well-established reflective language games for evaluating, re-authorizing, rejecting and changing practices; critique is a key practice for examining, evaluating and changing practices of discourse or of institutionality.[5] Practical philosophy is precisely this practice of reflective governance of the interpretation, application and reformulation of norms. Practical philosophy is precisely a concern with the governance of norms when they are problematic and cannot be simply deductively followed or applied. Practical philosophy as the cultivation of practical wisdom, *phronesis*, is precisely concerned with the communal reflective formulation of normative orders and their articulation with the variety of circumstances and situations. Practical philosophy is grounded in the recognition that any symbolic formulation of a norm, especially in written language, is confined to an abstract generality in its formulation such that its interpretation and application, even its understanding, depends on a more situated mediating judgment.

Against Theory

However, what is exemplary about both Hunter and Fish is their attempt to lower the philosophical stakes, to substitute *phronesis* for frenzy, to substitute mundane, practical, and specific forms of reasoning for the constant escalation by humanism into a semi-hysterical and wholly predictable binary between instrumental reason and transcendental reason. As Foucault declared in:

> … a document written and read by Foucault at a press conference in June, 1981 on the plight of the Vietnamese boat people: 'We must refuse the division of labor that is often proposed to us: between individuals who become indignant and speak out; and governments which reflect and act.' (Miller, 1993, p. 453)

By invoking the tradition of practical philosophy, I too wish to reject this liberal binary between individual and governmentality. The issue is whether instituting a more mundane, 'less critical' genre of discourse about education inevitably leads to a conservative valorization of the status quo. If administrative *praxis* does contain its own mode of being then, does the lowering of the temperature by Fish and Hunter in fact mean repressing or abandoning other modes of being, other values, other social goods? And where are they themselves standing in making these suggestions? Are they caught in a performative contradiction of some sort?

Hanna Fenichel Pitkin concludes her *Wittgenstein and Justice* with this reflection on the relationship between accepting the conventionality of our practices and how we should view change:

Thus, when Wittgenstein says that our forms of life must be accepted, that is not the same as saying that our lives as we lead them must be accepted, that our ways of theorizing about them must be accepted. Rather it suggests, as Cavell says, 'that criticism of our lives is not to be prosecuted in philosophical theory, but continued in the confrontation of our lives with their necessities'. It is not that we cannot change our concepts or our habits or our institutions; but that not every change is possible, and philosophizing will not change them. If they are to change, we must change them in our actions, in our lives; and ultimately that means that we cannot change them in isolation. (Pitkin, 1972, p. 340)

Thus, one of the tasks of this thesis will be to try to forge a voice that is worldly yet does not disavow, deny or repress the desire, need or grounds for change, a voice that acknowledges the contingency and conventionality of our practices and discourses but does not resign itself to this present, thereby ascribing inevitability and necessity to the present. Being realistic does not mean being fatalistic or passive.

Audience Expectations

I am acutely conscious of the way this text must conform to the conventions and standards of academic scholarship, that it can only be responsible to its occasion by 'meeting' these standards—if possible. Yet I am also acutely sensible to the fact that this text does not describe or prescribe nor enact any new classroom procedures for ABE (Adult Basic Education).[6] Many of my colleagues would see it as a self-indulgent 'wank'; a text that is more an act of selfish masturbation than healthy communicative intercourse with a readership. Ah! there's the rub: the readership ... Just who *is* the reader of this text? Perhaps it really is only me! Perhaps the examiners of this thesis are just third parties, voyeurs, looking over my shoulder— not the imagined readership at all. Perhaps this really is just a therapeutic text, an exercise in banishing, discharging the demons, ghosts and obsessions accumulated over years of teaching. Perhaps this text is just a way of unblocking congealed arteries and re-establishing the flow of good *phronesis* in my own practice. A retreat, a re-tread.

Of course, for ideas to function as reflection, as maxims, as resources for coping and making sense of events, as touchstones for formulating practices or actions, as horizons for orienting evaluations and assessments, as provocations to thinking— all this is one thing. But none of this adds up to a canonic academic PhD text. A modern PhD demands a central metanarrative depicting the growth of knowledge by expounding and justifying a technical metadiscourse (call it the logical form(ul)ation of concepts). So, although continually tempted by the sublime mirage of an a-modernist (pre- or post-modern) PhD, a text that systematically avoids positing an Archimedian point of view, that evades the logocentrism of 'the transparent word', the 'pure word' or 'the final word', I hereby acknowledge and pledge that I will address 'the claims of reason': the claims of coherence, consistency, evidence, and unity—just like Cavell!

Prefacing by Stealth

This thesis is, thus, my effort to 'let be' deeper horizons of answerability for our own *praxis* and discourse and for our students; horizons that are more elusive, not as readily inscribed in the form of institutional rules or boundaries. Already, I hope, you begin to sense the work of my text, the company it aspires (pretends) to keep, the words it fingers and looks to polish for reuse, the conceptual cloth it hopes to weave, the modes of reading it invokes and invites. And so, having begun with the notorious opening paragraphs of a contemporary philosophical text prefacing itself, let's retrieve an even more famous Prefacing of a philosophical text as a way of adducing the conventions and expectations of a preface and at the same time meditating on its status in philosophical prose. Here is the first paragraph of Hegel's *Phenomenology of Spirit* in which, drawing on his rigorous training in rhetoric, he discusses the paradoxicality of philosophical prefacing:

> An explanation, as it customarily precedes a book in a preface—about the purpose the author had in mind in writing it, or about the motivations and the relationships that the author sees his work entertaining to earlier or contemporary treatments of the same topic—such an explanation seems not only superfluous for a philosophical text but by the very nature of the matter even inappropriate and counterpurposeful. For the manner and the content of what could conveniently be said about philosophy in a preface—like a historical *indication* of the tendency, standpoint, the general argument and results, or like a connection between the conflicting claims and assurances about the truth—, these things cannot be valid given the way philosophical truth is to be depicted. (Hegel, 1910, p. 1)

Yet, just as Hegel is condemned to write precisely what he insists is superfluous, namely, to foreshadow the general topic, purpose, point, standpoint and relationship to other views and texts within the same domain, so too I hope I have hereby (indirectly and perversely) also fulfilled these self-same generic requirements of prefacing.

Notes

1. Aside from a few minor stylistic improvements, the Preface that follows, was written during 1994–5 and is unchanged from its final version as the preface to a PhD on Adult Basic Education (McCormack, 2000).
2. The feel of that style of philosophizing is re-captured for me in David Woods (1990) laconic remark:

> Much of what we think of as clarity and distinctness rests on topological hygiene, on good housekeeping: tidying spaces, mending fences, defining boundaries. If it were the business of philosophy to act as an under-labourer, and perhaps site manager, for the constructions of the sciences, it might be that the guidance

provided by such underlying schemas would prove invaluable. But ... . (Wood, 1990, p. xvi)

3. Different styles of prose embody different epistemological stances. In ancient poetics, Longinus nominated three prose styles: 'lofty, mean or lowly' ... The lofty prose is a prose of either the sublime intent on ecstasy or exciting and inciting an audience to passionate action. It is a prose of emotional intensity marked by what the rhetoricians call amplification, 'the rhetorical piling up of iteration' (Clark, 1957, p. 105). By contrast the lowly style is plain, simple and unadorned and thus appropriate to the statement of facts and proof. Philosophical texts especially in analytic philosophy are written in the low style, in what we would call a prosaic prose, not in a poetic prose. If we were to classify Cavell's prose (and the aspirations of my own prose in this thesis) in terms of this classical typography of three styles, Cavell is clearly subverting the genre of modern philosophy by mobilizing an elevated style marked by intensification, amplification and iteration.

4. Toulmin (1992, p. 175) notes that this:

   ... idea of 'starting again with a clean slate' has been as recurrent preoccupation of modern European thinkers as the quest for certainty itself. The belief that any new construction is truly *rational* only if it demolishes all that was there before and starts from scratch, has played a particular part in the intellectual and political history of France ... . The most spectacular illustration of this is the French Revolution.

5. For an exemplary articulation and recognition of contemporary cultural and social movements from a perspective that, like Hunter, draws on Wittgenstein and Foucault, see Tully (1995, 1999).

6. The author was deeply involved in the conceptual, pedagogic and institutional efforts to define Australian adult literacy and adult basic education as 'second chance education', efforts that peaked in the early 1990s (see McCormack, 1991).

References

Bourdieu, P. (1983) The Philosophical Institution, in: A. Montefiore (ed.), *Philosophy in France Today* (Cambridge, Cambridge University Press), pp. 1–8.

Cavell, S. (1979) *The Claim of Reason: Wittgenstein, skepticism, morality, and tragedy* (New York & Oxford, Oxford University Press).

Clark, D. (1957) *Rhetoric in Greco-Roman Education* (New York, Columbia University Press).

Dewey, J. (1922) *Human Nature and Conduct: An introduction to social psychology* (New York, The Modern Library).

Elbow, P. (1981) *Writing with Power: Techniques for mastering the writing process* (New York & London, Oxford University Press).

Fish, S. (1990) Rhetoric, in: F. Lentricchia & T. McLaughlin (eds), *Critical Terms for Literary Study* (Chicago, University of Chicago Press), pp. 203–222.

Gadamer, H. (1989) *Truth and Method*, 2nd revised edn.; trans. revised by J. Weinsheimer & D. G. Marshall (London, Sheed & Ward).

Hadot, P. (1995) *Philosophy as a Way of Life: Spiritual exercises from Socrates to Foucault*, ed. A. Davidson, trans. M. Chase, (Oxford & Cambridge, MA, Blackwell).

Halliday, M. (1985) *An Introduction to Functional Grammar* (London, Edward Arnold).

Halliday, M. (1987) Language and the Order of Nature, in: N. Fabb, D. Attridge, A. Durant & C. MacCabe (eds), *The Linguistics of Writing: Arguments between language and literature* (Manchester, Manchester University Press).

Hegel, G. (1910) *The Phenomenology of Mind*, trans. J. Baillie, (Oxford, Clarendon Press).

Hunter, I. (1994) *Rethinking the School: Subjectivity, bureaucracy, criticism* (Sydney, Allen & Unwin).

Kant, I. (1911) *Critique of Aesthetic Judgment*, trans. J. Meredith, (Oxford, Clarendon Press).

Kuhn, T. (1970) *The Structure of Scientific Revolutions* (Chicago, University of Chicago Press).

McCormack, R. (1991) Framing the Field: Adult literacies and the future, in: *Teaching English Literacy: A project of national significance on the preservice preparation of teachers for teaching English literacy Vol. 2.* (Darwin, NT, Centre for Studies of Language in Education) pp. 175–200.

McCormack, R. (2000) Adult Basic Education as Practical Philosophy: An hermeneutic account, (Unpublished PhD, James Cook University, Australia).

Miller, J. (1993) *The Passion of Michel Foucault* (New York, Simon & Schuster).

Pitkin, H. (1993) *Wittgenstein and Justice: On the significance of Ludwig Wittgenstein for social and political thought,* (Berkeley, CA & London, University of California Press).

Quintilian, M. (1921) *Institutio Oratoria,* Loeb Classical Library, ed. H. Butler (Cambridge, MA & London, Harvard University Press).

Rorty, A. (1983) Experiments in Philosophic Genre: Descartes' Meditations, *Critical Inquiry,* 9, pp. 545–564.

Rorty, R. (1980) *Philosophy and the Mirror of Nature* (Oxford, Basil Blackwell).

Scrag, C. (1989) *Communicative Praxis and the Space of Subjectivity* (Bloomington & Indianapolis, Indiana University Press).

Toulmin, S. (1992) *Cosmopolis: The hidden agenda of modernity* (Chicago, University of Chicago Press).

Tully, J. (1995) *Strange Multiplicity: Constitutionalism in an age of diversity* (Cambridge, Cambridge University Press).

Tully, J. (1999) The Agonic Freedom of Citizens, *Economy and Society,* 28:2, pp. 161–182.

Will, F. (1988) *Beyond Deduction: Ampliative aspects of philosophical reflection* (New York & London, Routledge).

Wittgenstein, L. (1963) *Philosophical Investigations,* trans. G. Anscombe, (Oxford, Basil Blackwell).

Wood, D. (1990) *Philosophy at the Limit* (London, Unwin Hyman).

3

Ong and Derrida on Presence:
A case study in the conflict of traditions

JOHN D. SCHAEFFER & DAVID GORMAN

In his 1988 work, *Whose Justice? Which Rationality?* Alasdair MacIntyre coined the phrase 'conflict of traditions.' His example of such a conflict was that between Thomism and the rationalism of the Scottish Enlightenment. MacIntyre showed how these two philosophies shared no common ground; there was no criterion of rationality or truth within either tradition that could adjudicate between them. On the contrary, MacIntyre says that modernity has rejected the truth claims of any tradition and instead has come to view them all as 'a series of falsifying masquerades' (MacIntyre, 1988, p. 395). But this view too, MacIntyre says, is a tradition. In other words, there is no escaping tradition, no way to achieve a coherent philosophical system without a history, without presumptions. Just as Gödel proved that no mathematical system can prove its own assumptions, so MacIntyre claims that no philosophical tradition can validate its own originating claims.

If there are two modern thinkers who might be said to represent a conflict of traditions, they must be Walter Ong and Jacques Derrida. Ong, who died in late 2003, was a Jesuit priest and a renowned scholar in the history of rhetoric; he is most famous for his studies of orality as the foundation of human thought and language. Derrida, who died in October of 2004, was a French-Algerian Jew whose philosophical career focused on the primacy of writing as the foundation of human thought and language. Timothy Clark has remarked that 'Ong's *Orality and Literacy* is one of the very small number of texts, along with Derrida's *Of Grammatology*, that change one's thinking about almost everything' (Clark, 2000, p. 242). Ong and Derrida occupy opposite ends of the spectrum of modern thought in virtually every respect: Ong the historian of rhetoric; Derrida the French *philosophe* who regards rhetoric as falsehood, albeit an inescapable one; Ong the enthusiastic logocentrist; Derrida the remorseless deconstructor of every certitude, every philosophical assumption. Ong has been seen also, and with good reason, as an apologist for Christianity, continually pointing out the implications of western philosophy's preoccupation with language for the Christian faith. Derrida, on the other hand, rejects every philosophical concept that undergirds the western theological tradition. Finally, Ong published heavily on media and culture, reporting on the transformations of human consciousness resulting from the advance of communications technology. Derrida analyzed communications technology with an aggressive hermeneutics of suspicion, finding little good in the emergence of mass communications and its corresponding mass markets.

Ong and Derrida seem to represent the most recent version of the ancient conflict of philosophy and rhetoric, but we hope to show that the seeming conflict between Ong and Derrida is not merely a conflict between rhetoric and philosophy, but a conflict within rhetoric and philosophy, more precisely, between Scholasticism and Rationalism, and between Aristotelian rhetoric and French neo-classical rhetoric.[1] Derrida's critique of presence within the western metaphysical tradition leads to his giving priority to rhetoric insofar as he assumes that rhetoric operates without 'timeless ideas,' as Newton Garver explains in his Preface to *Speech and Phenomena* (Derrida, 1973, pp. ix–xvii). Gayatri Spivak notes the same rhetorical-critical posture in Derrida's thinking. She says that for Derrida philosophical discourse is 'formal, rhetorical, figurative, discourse: a something to be deciphered' (Derrida, 1967, p. xxii). In short, for Derrida rhetoric is the belle-lettristic rhetoric of the *lycée* whose roots extend back to the 16th century. Rhetoric, in that sense, negates philosophical or metaphysical support for a transcendental signifier and invites a critique of all discourse that assumes the transcendental signifier.

While Derrida invokes belle-lettristic rhetoric to critique presence, Aristotelian rhetoric grounds Ong's affirmation of presence. Ong embraces the classical rhetorical tradition, while Derrida see philosophy collapsing back into belle-lettristic rhetoric. Its principles may be the cornerstone of his deconstructive work, but he regards the stone as a stumbling block, a scandal. We hope to place these two thinkers in historical perspective in order to illustrate that even within this conflict there is both shared and contested territory, but we will argue that the conflict itself must be figured in rhetorical, not philosophical, terms.

We begin where Aristotle says one should, at the beginning, more precisely, at the beginning of Ong's and Derrida's careers where each was concerned with the same issue: presence. The trajectory of their careers illustrates the difference between their ideas of rhetoric and how they pursued their implications. Ong and Derrida each invoke 'presence' to describe a key element in their accounts of the epistemological status of written texts. Yet each came to mean something entirely different by the term. For Ong 'presence' denotes the quintessentially human, that is, the presence of a human subject behind and in every human communication. For Derrida 'presence' denotes the signified as an essence, that is, the philosophically unworkable assumption that a signifier denotes a signified that is 'present,' full and entire, in the signifier. They seem to be using the term equivocally, but each meaning of presence grows from the same root. Tracing the emergence of their attitudes on 'presence', we find not only a common origin but also common concerns.

1. Some Preliminary Historical Observations

The episode in the history of rhetoric that formed the context of Ong's research was the so-called 'crisis of rhetoric' (1660–1700) that decisively reshaped the curriculum and pedagogy of Western Europe (de Dainville, 1978, pp. 195–96). The primary players in this crisis were the Jesuits and the French Jansenists. Originally, the Jesuit curriculum aimed at developing skill in disputation. This curriculum was codified in the Jesuit *Ratio studiorum* (1586), and, while the *Ratio* did not neglect writing, it preserved much of the orality that characterized ancient rhetoric. In fact, students spent half of the average school day either listening to or giving oral recitations or performances (Allen Farrell, 1938, pp. 346–48).

Peter Ramus (1515–1576), the subject of Ong's dissertation, initiated the crisis of rhetoric. Ong's *Ramus, Method and the Decay of Dialogue* (1958) details how Ramus created an art of 'dialectic' that purported to deal with probabilities (traditionally the province of rhetoric) in a fashion identical to logical demonstration, thus absorbing invention and organization into logic and leaving style as rhetoric's only legitimate concern—rhetoric as *belle lettres*. The Jesuit *Ratio studiorum* addressed Ramus by name: '[The teacher] should beware, however, of imitating Ramus by attaching an exaggerated importance to the logical element in Cicero. His speeches should be considered primarily from the rhetorical point of view' (quoted in Allen Farrell, 1938, p. 269). It was on 'the logical element in Cicero' that Ramus built his dialectic.

Ramism was only the beginning of the crisis, however. Jesuit pedagogy found an even more formidable opponent in the Jansenist school of Port-Royal. Port-Royal did away with rhetorical performance and focused almost exclusively on grammar and logic. While Port-Royal did not simplify the logical processes of thought as Ramus had done, it shares with Ramism a visually controlled model of thought, a divorce of discourse from the public arena, a profound mistrust of figurative language, and the relegation of rhetoric to ornamentation. Invention became private and interior, and arrangement was dominated by logic without concern for an audience. Port-Royal also shared Ramus's complete dependence on the printed book.

The Jesuits realized that the old *Ratio studiorum* needed modernizing. They replaced recitation and imitation with the memorizing of rules deduced in Cartesian fashion and illustrated with short passages. By 1700 Jesuit pedagogy was nearly indistinguishable from its competitors. Ong's and Derrida's careers need to be seen against the backdrop of the 'crisis of rhetoric'. Ong aimed to vindicate the original, oral nature of Jesuit pedagogy, while Derrida operated within the rationalist tradition that defined reason against classical rhetoric and relegated rhetoric to figurative discourse.

2. Ong on Voice in Ramus

Ong and Derrida each began their academic careers by illuminating the shortcomings of an influential figure who, they claimed, had imposed a false consciousness on Western thought. For Ong, the thinker was Ramus whose oversimplified spatial logic, he argued, had had catastrophic consequences for Western education and Western habits of thought. For Derrida, the thinker was Edmund Husserl, whose phenomenology eschewed metaphysical presuppositions, but who, Derrida argued, had failed to eliminate them entirely. Ong's attack on Ramus focuses on the latter's privileging of the visual, while Derrida's critique of Husserl focuses on the latter's privileging of the auditory. 'Presence' is the key term in Derrida's comments on

Husserl. Even though the term plays no role in Ong's discussion of Ramus, *Ramus, Method and the Decay of Dialogue* grounds Ong's case for the primacy of the oral in western consciousness, just as Derrida's *Speech and Phenomena* grounds Derrida's case for the primacy, or at least the irreducibility, of writing.

The index to Ong's *Ramus, Method and the Decay of Dialogue* lists only four references to dialogue but adds 'See dialectic.' There are thirty-one references to dialectic, some covering several pages. The orality that Ramism replaced was not the orality of the Socratic dialogue, but the orality of the college debating union. How then did Ramus contribute to a 'decay' of dialogue?

Ong's real quarrel with Ramism is that it pre-empted dialogue as a model for thought, whether dialogue is conceived as disputation, interrogation, or even conversation. Ong argued that Ramus's dialectic depended heavily upon visualization. Ramist textbooks are filled with diagrams and graphs that illustrate chains of binomial reasoning. Additionally, Ramus took the metaphor of the *topoi* (places) literally. He envisioned arguments (his term for any predication) generating and linking themselves in spatial fields. Drawing any subject from one topos to another would generate a multitude of propositions, but propositions not distinguished as probable or demonstrative.

Ramist dialectic thus produced predications by the dozens but without any concern for the truth of the premises. A classically trained disputant would think instinctively of the objections that could be raised by an opponent, but the Ramist formulated and linked propositions simply by going from place to place in Ramus's topical logic. There was, literally, no room for objection. Ong saw that Ramus had made thinking impersonal and isolate—a process that rigorously excluded any consideration of another point of view. Ramism, as Ong saw it, created a universe of contradictory discourses with no possibility of communication between them— discourse without dialogue.

Ramism's self-contained dialectic and concomitant isolation brought home to Ong the necessity of the 'other' for human rationality. The question he asked himself was 'How is the other present?' The answer was 'through orality.' Speech and hearing require an other as producer and receiver of sound. Sight, on the other hand, objectifies. To stare at something is to put it at a distance, to regard it as an object. For Ong, conceiving discourse as oral and auditory guarantees the presence of the other and guarantees it as the presence of a subject. It was precisely this presence that Ong found not present in Ramus. When Ong speaks of presence he means the presence of a subjective 'other' that focuses and directs a discourse, and that 'other' is most powerfully figured when thought is conceived as analogous to speaking and hearing.

3. Derrida on Voice in Husserl[2]

Derrida's treatment of the theme of presence found its fullest expression in *La Voix et le phénomène*, published in 1967 and translated into English under the title *Speech and Phenomena* in 1973. In this study Derrida concerns himself with the role of presence in Husserl's phenomenology, especially in relation to the motif of voice.[3]

Derrida's reflections upon presence and voice complement Ong's in many ways, indeed more ways than might be expected.

Derrida's thought is notoriously difficult to describe. Here is one preliminary formulation: Derrida assumes that metaphysics and metaphor come to largely the same thing, as his 'White Mythology' illustrates. If this is right, then Husserl's phenomenological project, which consists of describing aspects of experience without metaphysical presuppositions, is doomed from the start. Metaphors and other figures are too pervasive in language ever to be eliminated from a piece of discourse of any extent or detail. But any description of the phenomenological sort will involve an extended, detailed piece of discourse. Thus, on Derrida's assumption, metaphysics is ineliminable because metaphor is ineliminable.

Husserl's undertaking in the first of his *Logical Investigations* (1900–1901) is to sort out those elements of language that are essentially, ideally, and objectively meaningful from those that are only contingently, derivatively, or subjectively so. Derrida traces, first, the relation of voice to intention in Husserl. Husserl distinguishes between two categories of linguistic sign: 'expressive' signs, which are meaningful in the first (essential) way, and 'indicative' signs, which are not, and thus belong to the second category. Derrida follows the steps by which Husserl sets up a contrast between the two, noting the correlations established en route: expressive signs are those that are animated by an intention (or to put it literally, what they express is an intention), whereas indicative signs are mere marks that have no essential connection to conscious intent. Judging by Husserl's examples and images, the paradigm case of indicative signification is a piece of writing, whereas expressive signification is typically associated with the voice. Derrida shows that when Husserl attempts to describe expressive signs he turns to the metaphor of a voice speaking as if to itself. There is no spatial or temporal distance between the word spoken and the intention that speaks through it.

The difficulty that Derrida locates here is that the purpose of linguistic signs is precisely to carry expression across time and space; the very structure of the sign, as Husserl describes it, involves material embodiment, even if meaning itself is described as ideal, non-spatial, and non-temporal. He describes the ideal (or 'expressive') sign as existing in a changeless, extensionless medium. To introduce the possibility of spatial and temporal distance is to adulterate its ideality. And yet this possibility is the condition of every actual sign: the very purpose of actual signs is to compensate for non-proximity, to carry a message across temporal and spatial gaps (otherwise signs would not be needed). Therefore the Husserlian conception— which however is the paradigm of Western metaphysics—stands revealed as a fantasy. Signification always involves mediation, repetition, and distance rather than pure presence. There cannot be, finally, two kinds of signs, an expressive type that includes truly meaningful signs and indicative signs that serve as a useful but inessential supplement: 'in the end the need for indications simply means the need for signs' (Derrida, 1973, p. 42).

After deconstructing Husserl's idea of intention, Derrida turns to Husserl's key term 'presence,' analyzed in *The Phenomenology of Internal Time-Consciousness* (1905–1910; pub. 1928; Husserl, 1964). Husserl implicitly projects the present moment as an undivided unity imagined as an inner voice speaking to itself, as it is in the *Investigations*. In the *Phenomenology*, however, Husserl finds that, far from being a pure unity, the concept of the present moment has quite a complex structure, suggesting, as Derrida puts it, that 'the punctuality of the [present] instant is a myth, a spatial ... metaphor, an inherited metaphysical concept, or all that at once' (Derrida, 1973, p. 61). In upshot, Derrida argues that Husserl's model of meaning is compromised.

Derrida claims that Husserl's notion of pure expressiveness is impossible because meaning implies intentionality, and intention implies an ideal, a meaning which is so to speak 'face-to-face' with the meaning-intention. Even interior monologue formulates an intended meaning that implies an objective meaning that stands outside the intended meaning. There can be no pure expressiveness because meaning is never purely expressive. This analysis resembles Ong's claim that thinking in language requires an other. Ong would certainly agree that there can be no purely expressive interior monologue composed of a private language.

Derrida now pushes deeper into territory usually seen as Ong's province: an oral analogue or prototype for language. If expression is always inhabited and animated by meaning (*bedeuten*), as wanting to say, this is because, 'for Husserl, the *Deutung* (the interpretation or understanding of the *Bedeutung*) can never take place outside of oral discourse (*Rede*)' (Derrida, 1973, p. 33). Thus Derrida argues that, if meaning implies intentionality, it also implies orality. Husserl's phenomenology of language presupposes a concept of meaning that requires the presence of a person who consciously intends to mean something. Derrida's account of this resembles Ong's account of dialogue, in that both accounts require an other for meaning to arise in the subject. For Ong, this insight constitutes a critique of Ramism; for Derrida it marks a fault line in Husserlian phenomenology. It is significant that at this point Derrida's idea of 'presence' is congruent with Ong's: the presence of another person, an other whose presence is required by the meaning of meaning. Derrida now proceeds from this implied presence of the other to the presence attributed to the signified. (That is, in the parlance of structural linguistics favoured by Derrida, the content of a sign.)

Derrida claims that Husserl's account of expressive signs requires that the movement from conscious thought or intention to private language be instantaneous. But, on the basis of Husserl's own later analysis, Derrida denies that such simultaneity can exist; the presence of the self-reflective mind can never be entirely in the present (Derrida, 1973, pp. 60–69). On the contrary, even an interior monologue is infiltrated by temporality and thus involves 'indication' (not pure expression) even within the self. 'When the second person does emerge in inner language, it is a fiction' (Derrida, 1973, p. 70). This sounds remarkably similar to Ong's contention in 'The Writer's Audience is only a Fiction' that the mind requires an other even to think to itself, and indeed Derrida agrees, although he does not view the matters as Ong does; 'and fiction,' Derrida continues, 'after all, is only fiction. [... T]his is only a false communication, a feigned communication' (Derrida, 1973, p. 70). Ong might ask, 'false compared to what?' For Derrida the necessity of the other is a scandal, that is, the rhetoricality of language is a scandal. If the internal dialogue is not pure, then it must be false.

Derrida agrees with Ong that the other is absolutely necessary for meaningful signification to occur, even in an interior monologue, but if this necessary other is coupled with an oral/auditory model of communication where meaning is instantaneous and complete, it means that the signified can be fully present in the signifier (the material form taken by a sign as opposed to its content). This conclusion in turn is the foundation of Western metaphysics, which is the ultimate object of Derrida's critique. Because he finds that the oral/auditory model takes no account of the repeatability (or, as he prefers, 'iterability') of signs that constitutes communication, he urges a writer/reader model as a counterbalance. Here especially we can see that Ong and Derrida draw very different conclusions from at least partially congruent analyses. Ong uses the oral/auditory model to establish an epistemology grounded in dialogue and dialectic. Derrida uses the writer/reader model to unsettle that epistemology and to emphasize the irreducibility of the material signifier to an ideal signified.

4. Ong and Derrida on Metaphor

Nothing better illustrates the apparent gap between Ong and Derrida than their writings on metaphor. In them we can see the philosophical, indeed epistemological, abyss that opens between Ong's foundationalism and Derrida's antifoundationalism. Yet this abyss opens, as it were, on common ground: rhetoric. But, if we may strain the metaphor a little more, Ong and Derrida stand on opposite sides of an historical divide that provided the first fissure in that abyss.

Ramus and Port-Royal reduced rhetoric to a study of figurative language. A good example the French Enlightenment's attitude toward figurative language can be found in Dominique Bouhours's *La manière de bien penser dans les ouvrages d'esprit* (1687). He says 'Metaphors are like transparent veils which allow us to see what they cover; or like carnival masks under which one recognizes the person disguised' (Bouhours, 1687/1771, p. 17). Metaphors, in other words, do not communicate any truth that cannot be communicated without them. They are purely decorative, and philosophy can and ought to do without them. Derrida assumes that metaphor is a rhetorical use of language. Hence to philosophize is to speak non-rhetorically and non-metaphorically. His critique focuses on whether this non-metaphorical, philosophical discourse is possible.

In 'White Mythology: Metaphor in the Text of Philosophy' (first published in 1971) Derrida painstakingly peels away the metaphorical layers of the Enlightenment's signature metaphor: light = reason, knowledge, and/or truth. Derrida begins by dismissing all attempts to philosophize about metaphor, because there can be no account of metaphor that is not itself metaphorical, and because those metaphors would not be included in the account. Derrida fastens on another aspect of the paradox of metaphor. He asks '[w]hat logos as metaphor might be?' (Derrida, 1982, p. 228). He answers by pointing out the duplicity in the word 'sense,' which can apply to a signified (a non-spatial, a-temporal content) as well as to a signifier (which is sensible, that is, open to the senses). Because of this dualism at the heart of meaning, Derrida concludes that philosophy cannot deal with metaphor at all.

And by 'philosophy' he means rational discourse uncontaminated by metaphor, that is, uncontaminated by rhetoric, philosophy's impure twin. To deal with metaphor, rhetoric is all there is, and so he decides to use it against itself.

Derrida claims the duplicity of metaphor is the result of *mimesis*. In language redolent of Bouhours's, Derrida says 'metaphor indeed belongs to *mimesis*, to the fold of *physis*, to the moment when nature, itself veiling itself, has not yet refound itself in its proper nudity, in the act of its propriety' (Derrida, 1982, p. 241). Derrida means that propriety, the proper meaning, is not a given from which the metaphor deviates, but a meaning that must be found again in the metaphor even as the metaphor discloses the nakedness of nature by 'veiling' it, that is, covering it over in other language through which nature's nakedness is still visible.

Derrida argues next that metaphor's riskiness, its inherent capacity for missing things, is bound to an absence. He takes Aristotle's example: 'sow' is a word meaning to cast seed, but there is no word for the motion of the sun sending out its rays, so we can transfer the 'sowing' of the seed to the sun. But Derrida points out that we have never *seen* the sun sowing rays. Rather we transfer the meaning of 'sowing' to the shining of the sun, and this transference is mimetic. Derrida concludes '[t]he genius of *mimesis*, thus, can give rise to a language, a code of regulated substitutions, the talent and procedures of rhetoric, the imitation of genius, the mastery of the ungraspable' (Derrida, 1982, pp. 244–45). Here again Derrida identifies metaphor with rhetoric, but he seems at first to be articulating a theory of creativity that will make room for metaphor. His next question, however, reveals his attitude toward rhetoric and metaphor: 'Under what conditions,' he asks, 'would one always have one more trick ... up one's sleeve?' (Derrida, 1982, p. 245).

True to the tradition of French rationalism, Derrida considers metaphor a trick, but in the rest of 'White Mythology' he argues that all philosophical discourse falls victim to the trick of metaphor. That trick, it turns out, involves language, vision, and presence. The primacy of vision is built into the metaphor with which the Enlightenment described itself: light. Derrida says:

> Everything, in the discourse on metaphor, that passes through the sign *eidos*, with its entire system, is articulated with the analogy between the vision of the *noûs* and sensory vision, between the intelligible sun and the visible sun. The determination of the truth of the Being in presence passes through the detour of this tropic system. (Derrida, 1982, pp. 253–54)

Eidos is the Greek word for 'image,' that is, for something visible. An idea is something visible in the mind for which a proper word is thought to exist. In formulating this account of idea, however, one is already using a visual metaphor for thought. Furthermore, this model of metaphor's relation to thought presumes a certain static presence, the 'thing' for which the image 'stands' and which the word expresses. Hence the 'light' of the Enlightenment presumes a presence, an idea and its corresponding 'thing,' a duality that is only a metaphor itself. The title of 'White Mythology' is a metaphor for the problem Derrida is uncovering: the light that informs Enlightenment epistemology is a metaphor itself, but its brightness covers up the absence behind it, that is, the myth of a presence, a signified without a signifier. Here 'presence' for Derrida is the presence of the to-be-signified, and it is a presence implicated in the visual model for metaphorical thinking that Derrida inherited from Bouhours and other 18th century philosophers and critics.

If Derrida's concept of metaphor derives from rationalism, Ong's derives from Aristotelian scholasticism and its Baroque development, as he shows in his 'Metaphor and the Twinned Vision' (1962). In this article, Ong grants that the concept of metaphor is grounded in vision. Ong takes the metaphoricity of language for granted. He summarily dismisses the problem of 'proper versus improper' meaning. The proper meaning, he says, is a signification 'which has a kind of priority, a prescriptive or presumptive right to the term for the simple reason that, in the hurly-burly of semantic activity, it somehow got prior hold on that term' (Ong, 1962, p. 41). Like Derrida, Ong grants that the 'proper' meaning is quite as metaphorical as any figurative meaning derived from it. For Derrida this is a scandal; for Ong it is a fact of life.

Ong's model of metaphor is visual but it is twinned vision, as the title of the article indicates. The 'twinning' occurs when the imagination sees two things simultaneously and makes a connection between them. This connection Ong calls a predication. To use Aristotle's example again, Ong would say that when we say the sun is sowing its beams we are really saying 'shining *is* sowing,' that is, sowing is predicated of the sun's shining. 'Shining' and 'sowing' are twinned in a single vision. To Derrida's claim that 'we never *see* the sun sowing' Ong would reply, 'yes, we do, but we see it simultaneously with the sun shining.' Derrida's analysis of metaphor depends upon a model of substitution, while Ong's depends upon a model of predication and restates the theory of metaphor developed by baroque theorists in the 16th and 17th centuries.[4] Those theorists, mainly Italian, developed their ideas of metaphor in opposition to French rationalism's denial that metaphors conveyed any significant meaning. In short, Derrida's and Ong's accounts of metaphor originate in different, in fact opposed, literary and philosophical traditions. The philosophical tradition with which Derrida is engaged emerged in opposition to the Scholastic and baroque tradition within which Ong writes, and while Derrida is exposing the failure of Rationalism to reach its goal of non-metaphorical discourse, he does not hold any brief for the theory of metaphor that tradition replaced. Ong does.

The discussion of metaphor sets in starkest contrast the difference between Ong and Derrida. Both are criticizing the rationalist account of metaphor, but while Derrida argues that nothing is at the centre of metaphor, Ong argues that being is at the centre of metaphor and is so in a very literal sense. While Derrida claims that there is no presence, no signified, that has a proper meaning, Ong claims that the proper meaning is only a convention of usage. Finally, Derrida claims that since there is no proper meaning, there is no being in metaphor in the sense that nothing (no thing) can simply be itself. Ong claims that being is present in every metaphor, but dynamically, that is, as a predication, a verb, not as a subsistent, a thing. Ong's logocentrism is grounded in a Scholastic metaphysics and a baroque aesthetics that can be traced to Aquinas's formula that 'being is analogous,' while Derrida claims that the failure of modern philosophy to escape metaphor dooms it to a metaphysics of presence that modern linguistics has discredited. Let us turn now to the genealogy of these two concepts of presence and non-presence. We shall discover that they are closely related.

5. Ong and (or, versus) Derrida

One never has to read far in Ong to encounter a phonocentric (sound-centered) streak or a logocentric (speech-centered) one, or both, as the quickest perusal of *The Presence of the Word* will show.

> Thus even when we conceive of communication as a transaction more funda-
> mental than speech, we still conceive of it with reference to the world of
> sound where speech has its being, and thus attest in a reverse way to the
> paramountcy of sound and the oral-aural world in communication ... .
> Words are always primarily spoken things—writing transposes speech
> to a spatial medium, but the language so transposed has come into
> existence in the world of sound. (Ong, 1964, p. 3)

And he adds later, 'We have been slow to note, although the linguistic experts remind us constantly of it now, that writing is a derivative of speech, not vice versa, and that speech in its original state has nothing to do with writing' (Ong, 1964, p. 21).[5]

All the thematic correlations identified by Derrida in Western thought about language—involving such notions as voice, writing, death, presence, fullness, etc.—positively flourish in Ong. 'One cannot have voice without presence, at least suggested presence. And voice ... being the paradigm of all sound for man, sound itself thus of itself suggests presence' (Ong, 1964, p. 114). And:

> Although sound itself is fleeting, ... what it conveys at any instant of its
> duration is not dissected but caught up in the actuality of the present ... .
> Although ... sound perishes each instant that it lives, the instant when it
> does live is rich. Through sound we can become present to a totality
> which is a fullness, a plenitude. [... S]ound and hearing have a special
> relationship to our sense of presence. When we speak of presence in its
> fullest sense—the presence which we experience in the case of another
> human being, which another person exercises on us and which no object
> or living being less than human can exercise—we speak of something that
> surrounds us, in which we are situated. (Ong, 1964, pp. 129–30)

The conceptual affiliations that Derrida finds hidden in Husserl's discourse and that he reveals as secretly governing Husserl's thought are expressly embraced by Ong.

In *Orality and Literacy*, Ong cites Derrida's work several times, offering some comments on it and devoting a more extended discussion to deconstruction generally and to the various theorists whom Ong calls 'textualists' (Ong, 1982, pp. 165–70). Ong does not mention *Speech and Phenomena*. He addresses only *Of Grammatology* and *Writing and Difference*, and the Derrida discussed in *Orality and Literacy* is exclusively a fellow-historian of literacy, although one whose otherwise commendable work suffers from certain limitations and confusions.

Ong says that, at its strongest, the analysis offered by Derrida and other 'textualists' serves to remind us that much thought about language has been led astray by a 'bias' toward written forms resulting in the assimilation of orality to literacy, leading to the general assumption that there simply is a one-to-one correspondence between spoken words and written words on the basis of which:

> ... the naive reader presumes the prior existence of an extra-mental referent which the word presumably captures and passes on through a kind of pipeline to the psyche ... . Derrida excoriates this metaphysics of presence. He styles the pipeline model 'logocentrism' and diagnoses it as deriving from 'phonocentrism,' that is, from taking the logos or sounded word as primary, and thereby debasing writing by comparison with oral speech. Writing breaks the pipeline model because it can be shown that writing has an economy of its own so that it cannot simply transmit unchanged what it receives from speech. Moreover, looking back from the break made by writing, one can see that the pipeline is broken even earlier by spoken words, which do not themselves transmit an extra-mental world of presence as through transparent glass. Language is structure, and its structure is not that of the extra-mental world. (Ong, 1982, pp. 166–67)

In short, Ong concludes, 'In breaking up with phonocentrism and logocentrism, Derrida is performing a welcome service, in the same territory that Marshall McLuhan swept through his famous dictum, "The medium is the message"' (Ong, 1982, p. 167). While passages like these show how mistaken it would be to assume that Ong himself is merely a logocentrist, the terms of his praise will inevitably trouble Derrideans, who would not at all accept Derrida as a kind of latter-day McLuhan. A deconstructionist also would reject Ong's term 'extra-mental,' since that suggests that there are transparent connections between linguistic signs and things inside the mind.

Ong also expresses reservations about Derrida, deconstruction, and 'textualism' at various points in *Orality and Literacy*. A major criticism has to do with a favourite point of Ong's, namely that the evolution of Western culture involved more than a shift from orality to literacy. Ong stresses that a second revolution followed the emergence of script, that of print, by which 'writing was deeply interiorized' in consciousness (Ong, 1982, p. 97). For Ong, drawing a distinction between chirographic and typographic literacy would be a step toward methodological self-awareness for Derrida and others: 'Deconstruction is tied to typography rather than, as its advocates seem often to suppose, merely to writing' (Ong, 1982, p. 129). Ong is far from denying that the logical inconsistencies and paradoxes that deconstructionists seek out in texts are to be found there. His point is that the significance that Derrida and others attribute to these undeniable qualities indicates the very limited perspective of deconstruction.

> What leads one to believe that language can be so structured as to be perfectly consistent with itself, so as to be a closed system? There are no

closed systems and never have been. The illusion that logic is a closed system has been encouraged by writing and even more by print ... . The work of the deconstructionists ... derives its appeal in part from historically unreflective, uncritical literacy. (Ong, 1982, p. 169)

Let us now view the conflict from a Derridean-deconstructive viewpoint. While it is imaginable that Derrida could view Ong as a fellow-traveller in a number of respects, it would always be with the qualification that each of Ong's contributions are shallower and less thorough. To return to the example of McLuhan and his slogan 'The medium is the message'. To the extent that, historically, there is indeed a dubious hierarchy at work in Western thought in which medium has been contrasted with message at the expense of the medium, Derrida could hold that McLuhan was doing useful and as it were proto-deconstructive work in problematizing this hierarchy, in claiming that the distinction between the two is less than clear-cut and that they have a coequal status (as in, the medium = the message). But for a deconstructor this would be no more than one step in the right direction; deconstruction entails a programmatic questioning of all such hierarchies, which covertly structure all concepts.

Much of what we have explored so far is intelligible as exemplars of the orality versus literacy paradigms that both Ong and Derrida investigate. So far we have looked at these as paradigms of epistemology. But shortly after publishing his book on Ramus, Ong found a new dimension to his investigation of orality and presence: existentialism. In his *Walter J. Ong's Contributions to Cultural Studies*, Thomas J. Farrell points out that Ong's thinking took a decisive turn toward presence when he read Martin Buber's *I and Thou*. In this book Buber argues that the human subject is existentially oriented toward another, and not 'the other' but a 'thou,' another subject with whom one enters into intimate relation. The mode of that relation, according to Buber, is dialogue. While not precluding dialogue in writing, Buber foregrounds oral dialogue because the voice indicates an immediate human presence. Intimacy is easier because the other is here, heard, that is, present.

For Ong, orality became more than the basis of an epistemology. It became the basis of an ethics, indeed of a whole existentialist philosophy. Under Buber's tutelage Ong made orality the foundation of his paradigm of human being-in-the-world. Orality thus carries a great deal more freight for Ong than writing does for Derrida. The presence that inhabits Ong's concept of orality is the presence of the human not merely the presence of the signified.

Perhaps their treatments of writing provide an insight into their later thinking about presence. This observation is itself suggestive, since something that Ong and Derrida hold in common is that they both link writing to presence. Although *The Presence of the Word* seems quite provocatively entitled from the deconstructive perspective, the remarks that Ong actually makes about presence in these lectures suggest that he is working with the notion of presence that he inherited from Buber rather than the one Derrida scrutinizes in *Speech and Phenomena*: 'To present himself, man must find the presence of another or others. Man's life-world is ... a world not of presence but of presences ... . Situated among objects, a person may indeed find them interesting, but he responds only to other persons, other presences, who are not objects' (Ong, 1964, p. 295).

The relation of time and space to presence is likewise entirely different in Derrida and Ong. For Ong temporality is the essential quality of the linguistic sign in its oral mode—that is, the presence of the oral word is a temporal one; in contrast, the written word is present spatially, since the introduction of literacy brings with it a transition to a visual framework for the use of language. But for Derrida, as we have seen, time and space are both categories that *contrast* with that of presence: the fact that a sign can function across time and space—and that it is a condition of its being a sign that it can do so—simply means that it cannot partake of pure presence. It is hard to see how to compare two such different employments of these concepts.

6. Analogues for Intellect and Conflict of (and in) Traditions

One thing about Ong and Derrida is quite clear: both are essentially historians. They are historians, however, of different but overlapping phenomena. Ong is an historian of culture who is concerned with the predominance of one or another of the human senses. Ong traces a kind of spectrum (or musical scale) as human culture has moved from the purely auditory, to scribal, to print, to electronic communication. Across this spectrum (or scale), hearing and seeing compete for dominance as the 'analogue for intellect,' that is, the sensory model for how a culture conceives thinking itself. Ong traces the tradeoffs that occur in culture and consciousness in response to changing communication technologies. From this perspective Derrida is essentially someone reading the history of philosophy solely (and Ong would say unconsciously) in the light of the contemporary state of communicative technology—namely print. Derrida, in Ong's view, has taken what Ong calls the 'hypervisualism' of modern philosophy as normative, and he has found its own metaphysical assumptions insupportable.

Derrida saw himself as a philosopher who used an historical approach. He wished to articulate the often hidden or underlying pattern of hierarchically organized binaries that constitute 'Western metaphysics' and thus also constitute the framework of all Western thinking. Derrida's purpose in articulating this system, showing it at work in the discourse of various philosophers, theoreticians, and writers generally, is to prepare the way for a genuine alternative which is unthinkable within the enclosure of metaphysics. From Derrida's perspective, Ong's ideas would be a mixture of the revolutionary and regressive: revolutionary in that they mount a formidable historical critique of technology compatible with Derrida's own critique of *techne*, but certainly regressive in that Ong defends the logocentrism at the heart of Western metaphysics and the primacy of orality at the heart of logocentrism.

Ong's work certainly deserves the attention of Derrideans who might try to follow Ong's paradigm of dialogue and begin one with him. A particularly likely beginning point lies in Ong's emphasis on the way that certain texts combine oral and literate modes in complicated and ambiguous ways. One example is Plato's writing, which Ong expressly advances as a challenge for deconstructive analysis in *Orality and Literacy* (pp. 167–68). The most challenging and ambiguous case of all, however, is the Bible. Ong's 'Maranatha: Death and Life in the Text of the Book' simply calls out to be read in juxtaposition with Derrida's *The Gift of Death*. The comparison suggests the ethical implications that emerge from a 'conflict of traditions' that originally seemed preoccupied with epistemological issues and the analogues for intellect imbedded in them.[6]

Ong's 'Maranatha' grapples with Christianity's profound commitment to the Word as a metaphor for Christ's divinity, while Derrida grapples with Christianity as a mediator between orgiastic, demonic paganism on the one hand and Platonism and neo-Platonism on the other. Despite this difference, both texts deal with issues of openness and response but figured in different analogues for intellect. Ong asks, 'How far does the reading of the Bible today call for reestablishing relationship between the text and reader distinctive of the highly oral culture of the biblical age?' (Ong, 1977, p. 270). Derrida's account of response is figured visually: 'the exposing of the soul to the gaze of another person, of a person as transcendent other, as an other who looks at me' (Derrida, 1995, p. 25). Derrida conceives of God as an other who fixes one in his gaze, who sees all that is in the soul. And it is a silent gaze. He identifies it, with the silence of Dasein, and later describes God as he who 'holds me in his gaze and in his hand while remaining inaccessible to me' (Derrida, 1995, pp. 32, 33). Furthermore Derrida says that language or speech neutralizes the uniqueness of the individual's response: 'The first effect or first destination of language therefore involves depriving me of, or delivering me from, my singularity' (Derrida, 1995, p. 60). Ong, on the contrary, asserted throughout his career that language in a living voice constitutes the paradigm of the individual's response to the other. Derrida's 'religion without religion,' as Caputo calls it, is grounded in a visual analogue for the person's encounter with the wholly other, while Ong's personalized Christianity is grounded in the oral/aural analogue for that encounter. Nowhere is this clearer than in how each interprets the story of Abraham's sacrifice of Isaac.

In *The Presence of the Word* Ong invokes the Abrahamic story to illustrate how voice is the paradigmatic sign of presence. His interpretation is clearly indebted to Kierkegaard:

> Abraham knew God's presence when he heard His 'voice.' ... As establishing personal presence, the word has immediate religious significance, particularly in the Hebrew and Christian tradition, where so much is made of a personal, concerned God ... . The divine presence irrupts *into* time and space and 'inhabits' them. Presence does not irrupt into voice. One cannot have voice without presence ... . [V]oice is not inhabited by presence as by something added; it simply conveys presence as nothing else can. (Ong, 1964, pp. 113–14, original emphasis)

For Ong the Abraham episode is essentially an aural event. It conforms perfectly to the model of response-to-the-other that he inherited from Martin Buber and ultimately from Kierkegaard.

Derrida's interpretation of this episode negates the personalism that permeates the Ong-Buber interpretation.[7] First he says that Abraham's response to God requires that he 'renounce his family loyalties, which amounts to violating his oath, and refuse to present himself before men. *He no longer speaks to them*' (Derrida, 1995, p. 62, emphasis ours). Derrida thus interprets the episode not as a response but as a silencing, adding, 'That at least is what the sacrifice of Isaac suggests.' Derrida proceeds to configure Abraham's sacrifice as a call to 'a duty not to respect, out of duty, ethical duty. One must behave not only in an ethical or responsible manner, but in a non-ethical, non-responsible manner, and one must do that in the name of duty, of an infinite duty, in the name of absolute duty' (Derrida, 1995, p. 67). Here Derrida is departing radically from Kierkegaard's interpretation. Kierkegaard claimed that Abraham transcended ethical duty and moved into the realm of the religious, the response to the holy. Derrida, on the other hand, is construing the episode to mean that Abraham's relation to God is still ethical, only a kind of Nietzschean transvalued ethics. Derrida goes so far as to say that Abraham is 'in a relationship to God—a relationship without relation because God is absolutely transcendent' (Derrida, 1995, pp. 72–73). And then continues that 'what can be said about Abraham's relation to God can be said about my relation without relation to *every other (one) as every (bit) other [tout autre comme tout autre]*, in particular my relation to my neighbor or my loved ones' (Derrida, 1995, 78, original emphasis).[8] It is difficult to imagine an interpretation of the Abraham/Isaac passage that would be more antithetical to Ong's and Buber's. Not only does Derrida deny that Abraham's 'relation' to God is religious or personal, he says that this 'relation without relation' is a paradigm for all other human relationships. In short, he claims that the personalism that Ong and Buber predicate generally of human relationships does not exist.

This conclusion might be last stage in an irreconcilable conflict of traditions, but in *Memoirs of the Blind* Derrida goes even further into what Ong calls 'hypervisualism'. *Memoirs of the Blind* is a commentary and catalogue of an art exhibition Derrida organized at the Louvre. He decided to display the Louvre's collection of drawings and paintings about blindness. That he would even choose such a subject shows the depths to which the visual permeated his thought. His exploration of the inherent contradictions of rationalism has led him from a critique of phenomenology to a denial of human intimacy, much more than simply a denial of a religious relation-ship as it is usually conceived. Ong, on the other hand, working within the oral/aural paradigm of classical and Renaissance rhetoric, quickly adapted that paradigm to the orally-controlled theology of Catholic Christianity. Is this finally the end point of the conflict of traditions?

In a very limited way, yes. But in another sense, no, at least not as long as one is conscious of the 'sense' that one chooses to figure as the analogue for intellect. This comparison of Ong and Derrida reveals the depth to which sensory metaphors are imbricated in their thinking and suggests that the real work of intellectual inquiry must now be, first, reflection upon the adequacy of these analogues and second, speculation about alternative analogues. In other words, the conflict between traditions (rhetoric and philosophy) depends upon conflicts *within* each tradition: classical versus belle-lettristic rhetoric and Scholasticism versus French rationalism. Interrogating these traditions for common ground would owe more to Ong's work than to Derrida's. Ong's understanding of the rhetorical tradition seems to give him more leverage on Derrida's visually-based critique of philosophy, than Derrida's philosophical critique gives on Ong's orally-based concept of rhetoric. While there might be space for dialogue at the level of epistemology and cultural critique, at the level of ethics and the way humans exist in the world, the space closes and the conflict between the traditions of rhetoric and philosophy—in this version between an orally-based personalism and a visually based post-modernism—seems irreconcilable as long as both sides maintain their characteristic analogues for intellect.

Notes

1. For a discussion of belle-lettristic rhetoric during the French Enlightenment see France, 1972. For a description of how rhetoric has been taught in France see Compère, 1985, pp. 193–204. To see how 17th century rhetoric has survived in France see Brown, 1927.
2. For a general discussion of Husserl and phenomenology, see Moran, 2000.
3. For a coherent explication of *Speech and Phenomena* see Lawlor, 2002. For a more critical analysis see Evans, 1991.
4. For a good account of the status of metaphor in French literary criticism, see Mazzeo, 1964, pp. 45–50.
5. For a revisionist approach to Ong's distinctions between orality, literacy and print, see Peters, 1998.
6. For a different discussion of religion in Derrida's thought see Caputo, 1997 especially pp. 281–331.
7. Derrida's interpretation of the Abraham and Isaac episode seems to be a concrete example of what he stated more abstractly in 'Faith and Knowledge: The two sources of "religion" at the limits of reason alone'. For an analysis that ties to synthesize voice and silence in *Fear and Trembling*, see Mackey, 1986, pp. 40–67.
8. For penetrating analyses of Derrida's thinking on 'otherness' in a religious context, see de Vries, 1999, pp. 96–108.

References

Bouhours, D. [1687] (1771) *La manière de bien penser dans les ouvrages d'esprit* (Paris, Libraire Associés).

Brown, W. R. (1927) *How the French Boy Learns to Write: A study in the teaching of the mother tongue* (Cambridge, MA, Harvard University Press).

Caputo, J. (1997) *The Prayers and Tears of Jacques Derrida: Religion without religion* (Bloomington, IN, Indiana University Press).

Clark, T. (2000) Deconstruction and Technology, in: N. Royle (ed.), *Deconstructions: A user's guide* (New York, Palgrave).

Compère, M.-M. (1985) *Du college au Lycée (1500–1850)* (Paris, Éditions Gallimard/Julliard).

de Dainville, F. (1978) *L'Éducation des Jésuites (XVI–XVIIIe siecle)* (Paris, Minuit).

Derrida, J. (1967) *Of Grammatology*, G. C. Spivak, trans. and pref. (Baltimore, MD, Johns Hopkins University Press).

Derrida, J. (1973) *Speech and Phenomena and other Essays on Husserl's Theory of Signs*, D. B. Allison, trans., N. Garver, pref. (Evanston, IL, Northwestern University Press).

Derrida, J. (1978) *Writing and Difference*, A. Bass, trans. (Chicago, University of Chicago Press).

Derrida, J. (1982) White Mythology: Metaphor in the text of philosophy, in: *Margins of Philosophy* A. Bass, trans. (Chicago, University of Chicago Press).

Derrida, J. (1993) *Memoirs of the Blind: The self-portrait and other ruins*, P-A. Brault & M. Naas, trans. (Chicago, University of Chicago Press).

Derrida, J. (1995) *The Gift of Death*, D, Wills, trans. (Chicago, University of Chicago Press).

Derrida, J. (1998) Faith and Knowledge: The two sources of 'religion' at the limits of reason alone, S. Weber, trans., in: J. Derrida & G. Vattimo (eds), *Religion* (Stanford, CA, Stanford University Press).

Evans, J. C. (1991) *Strategies of Deconstruction: Derrida and the myth of the voice* (Minneapolis, University of Minnesota Press).

Farrell, A. P. (1938) *The Jesuit Code of Liberal Education: Development and scope of the ratio studiorum* (Milwaukee, WI, Bruce Publishing).

Farrell, T. J. (2000) *Walter J. Ong's Contributions to Cultural Studies* (Cresskill, NJ, Hampton).

France, P. (1972) *Rhetoric and Truth in France: Descartes to Diderot* (Oxford, Clarendon Press).

Husserl, E. (1964) *The Phenomenology of Internal Time-Consciousness*, M. Heidegger, ed., J. S. Churchill, trans. (Bloomington, IN, Indiana University Press).

Lawlor, L. (2002) *Derrida and Husserl: The basic problem of phenomenology* (Bloomington, IN, Indiana University Press).

MacIntyre, A. (1988) *Whose Justice? Which rationality?* (Notre Dame, IN, University of Notre Dame Press).

Mackey, L. (1986) *Points of View: Readings of Kierkegaard* (Tallahassee, Florida State University Press).

Mazzeo, J. A. (1964) *Renaissance and Seventeenth-Century Studies* (New York, Columbia University Press).

Moran, D. (2000) *Introduction to Phenomenology* (New York, Routledge).

Ong, W. J. (1958) *Ramus, Method and the Decay of Dialogue: From the art of discourse to the art of reason* (Cambridge, MA, Harvard University Press).

Ong, W. J. (1962) Metaphor and the Twinned Vision, in: *The Barbarian Within, and Other Fugitive Essays and Studies* (New York, Macmillan).

Ong, W. J. (1964) *The Presence of the Word: Some prolegomena for cultural and religious history* (New Haven, CT, Yale University Press).

Ong, W. J. (1977) Maranatha: Death and life in the text of the book, in: *Interfaces of the Word: Studies in the evolution of consciousness and culture* (Ithaca, NY, Cornell University Press).

Ong, W. J. (1982) *Orality and Literacy: The technologizing of the word* (New York, Methuen).

Peters, J. S. (1998) Orality, Literacy, and Print Revisited, in: D. L. Weeks & J. Hoogestraat (eds), *Time, Memory, and the Verbal Arts: Essays on the thought of Walter Ong* (Cranbury, NJ, Susquehanna University Press).

de Vries, H. (1999) *Philosophy and the Turn to Religion* (Baltimore, MD, Johns Hopkins University Press).

4

Bridging Literary and Philosophical Genres: Judgement, reflection and education in Camus' *The Fall*

PETER ROBERTS

Introduction

Albert Camus has long been regarded as one of the most 'philosophical' of 20th century novelists. He laid no claim to the title 'philosopher' himself, and some have been quick to reinforce this view. Walter Kaufmann (1959), for example, in a discussion of existentialism and death, is rather dismissive of what he sees as Camus' two philosophical works: *The Myth of Sisyphus* (Camus, 1991) and *The Rebel* (Camus, 1953). Kaufmann endorses Henri Peyre's judgement of these books as 'not only contradictory, but confused and probably shallow and immature' (cited in Kaufmann, 1959, p. 87). After critiquing the concept of the absurd in *The Myth of Sisyphus*, Kaufmann concludes that 'Camus is a fine writer, but not a philosopher' (p. 90). Others have reached quite different conclusions. Thomas Hanna (1958), for instance, writing around the same time as Kaufmann, saw Camus as 'one of the most prophetic, persuasive, and hopeful moral philosophers of the mid-20th century' (p. viii). For Hanna, *The Myth of Sisyphus* provides a searching examination of some of the most important philosophical themes of Camus' age. *The Rebel*, too, has received high praise from others. Russell Ford (2004), for example, maintains that *The Rebel* is 'one of the most profound and under-studied pieces of political theory composed during the 20th century' (p. 86).

Kaufmann's focus is on Camus' non-fiction, and his assessment is of Camus *as* philosopher. When attention is paid to Camus' full corpus of published writings, however, it becomes possible to speak of *philosophical readings* of works that were not intended as works of philosophy. With this shift in focus, scholarship in the years following the publication of Kaufmann's essay would seem to suggest that for those seeking to address philosophical questions, much can be gained from reading Camus. Over the past half century, there has been sustained interest in the ethical, ontological, metaphysical, and aesthetic problems posed by Camus' novels, short stories, plays, and non-fiction writings. Camus, more than most accomplished novelists, enables his readers to bridge different genres of writing, thinking and being, linking the literary with the philosophical. For Hanna (1958), this 'interplay between the philosophical and literary concerns of Camus is largely responsible for the richness and value of his writings' (p. 35). Camus' reach into different fields has been equalled by few other writers of his generation. His work has been engaged by those concerned with politics (Cruickshank, 1960; Woolfolk, 1984; LeBlanc, 2004), psychology (Grobe, 1966), justice and human rights (Ford, 2004; Orme, 2007), colonialism and anti-colonialism (Vulor, 2000), film (Vines, 2003), and theology (Onimus, 1970; Skrimshire, 2006), among other domains. Camus' writings have also attracted comment from a number of educationists over the years (e.g. Denton, 1964; Greene, 1973; Oliver, 1973; Götz, 1987; Curzon-Hobson, 2003; Gibbons & Heraud, 2007; Marshall, 2007a,b; Weddington, 2007).

Of Camus' literary works, *The Fall* (Camus, 2000) is perhaps the most significant for those seeking to bridge literary and philosophical genres. Brian Fitch (1995) sees *The Fall* as Camus' 'finest achievement as a writer' (p. 122). Avi Sagi (2002) agrees that this is 'one of the deepest and most beautiful of Camus's works' (p. 131). The philosopher Robert Solomon (2004) describes the book as a 'brilliant quasi-religious novel' (p. 41). Others, as Hustis (2007) observes, have often seen the book as 'an earnest, yet tongue-in-cheek, response to the scathingly personal criticisms leveled at the Nobel-prize-winning author by his one-time friend and compatriot Jean-Paul Sartre' (p. 1). *The Fall* was, in fact, Sartre's favourite book by Camus. When asked why this was so, Sartre said it was because 'Camus put himself and hid himself entirely in that work' (Todd, 2000a, p. xx). My inclination, as this paper will elaborate, is with those who see *The Fall* as 'the most enigmatic of Camus' works' (Locke, 1967, p. 306). More than anything else, *The Fall* is characterised by ambiguity (Madden, 1966). Key early critics found the book complex, pessimistic and difficult to interpret (Hartstock, 1961, p. 357). Responses over subsequent decades have only added to the sense that this is a multi-layered work, demanding deep reflection on the part of the reader.

In the educational literature on Camus, little attention has been paid specifically to *The Fall*. This chapter celebrates *The Fall's* difficulties, arguing that in the complexities and ambiguities of the novel lie educational opportunities. The open-endedness of *The Fall*, it will be suggested, invites a form of philosophical reflection that is—or *may* be—educative. The chapter is structured in three parts. The first section provides a brief account of the origins, form and content of the book. This is followed by a closer examination of the last part of the novel, where the main character, Clamence, is shown to be at his most vulnerable and where his pedagogical method as a judge-penitent is described. The final section considers how Camus' distinctive blending of the literary with the philosophical prompts readers to reflect on themselves, their motivations and commitments, their relationships with others, and the very process of reflection itself.

The Fall: Genesis, Form and Content

The Fall grew out of a difficult period in Camus' life. When the book was published (as *La Chute*) in 1956, Camus was, as Olivier Todd (2000a, p. v) describes it, 'physically and psychologically exhausted' (p. v). He and Jean-Paul Sartre had had a very public falling out, the latter finding fault with Camus' political position in

The Rebel. (For further details on the conflict between Sartre and Camus, see Todd, 2000b.) Camus regretted the loss of Sartre's intellectual friendship, and he found himself at odds with a number of others in French literary circles. Camus' stance on the Algerian conflict did not mesh comfortably with Sartre's Marxist analysis of French colonialism, and when an all-out war erupted in the mid-1950s he was filled with horror. Camus embraced a vaguely defined ideal of a 'Mediterranean civilization', believing that 'more than a hundred years after the conquest of Algeria, white settlers were entitled to live there, just as much as the Arabs and Kabyles were' (p. v). His left-wing French colleagues branded him a 'reactionary', proclaiming him a traitor for his anti-communism and his refusal to align himself with Algerian nationalists (p. x). At this time, Camus' marriage to Francine Faure was also in trouble, and he was suffering from writer's block. He was ill, with the effects of tiredness, depression and TB all taking their toll (p. viii). He felt burnt-out and wondered what he had really accomplished in his life to date. His response was to begin writing some short stories, and this is how *The Fall* was born.

Todd (2000a) notes that in his early twenties, Camus had planned his writing in terms of cycles, each cycle comprising a novel, a play and an essay. One cycle, the Absurd, included *The Outsider* (Camus, 1983), *Caligula* (Camus, 1962) and *The Myth of Sisyphus* (Camus, 1991), while another, Revolt, was made up of *The Plague* (Camus, 1960), several plays and *The Rebel* (Camus, 1953). *The First Man* (Camus, 1996), the incomplete novel not published in English until several decades after Camus' untimely death in 1960, was intended to form part of a happier cycle (p. xix). *The Fall* was not planned as part of one of these cycles. It came into being more by accident, growing from story length to something approaching a short novel, driven along by creative energies Camus' felt he had lost. Difficult circumstances and intellectual isolation had taken Camus to the depths of despair, but they also provided fertile inspiration—and subject matter—for the work rapidly unfolding. *The Fall* is, as Hanna (1958) puts it, 'the most personal of Camus' works', but in some ways it is also 'the least revealing' (p. 219). There is much of Camus in the book, but *The Fall* is also a portrait of Sartre and his comrades in the French intelligentsia of the 1950s. At the same time, the ideas conveyed in the book are not merely an amalgamation of the views held by Camus, Sartre and other Parisian intellectuals at the time. *The Fall* is a complement to *The Outsider*, but there are arguably also echoes of Camus' other works in the book.

The complexity of *The Fall* is evident not only in its content but in its form. *The Fall* defies easy description. Some have even been reluctant to call *The Fall* a novel. At around 100 pages, some prefer to see it as a novella, or as a semi-autobiographical confession, or as a work of philosophy. David Madden (1966) captures some of the problems for those seeking to categorise this work:

> Only in the most liberal sense can Albert Camus' *The Fall* be called a novel. Camus himself never claimed it to be a novel as such. Although it has characteristics of the conventional novel, it is also similar in form and content to a long and personalized philosophical essay in the manner of Kierkegaard or of Plato's dialogues, the interlocutor's questions merely

implied. Seemingly a monologue, there are suggestions that it is more than a soliloquy. As an essay-novel, composed of anecdotes, epigrams, observations that include numerous ethical questions, poetic passages, and a faint story line, discernible in the progression of Jean-Baptiste's 'spiritual' transformation, *The Fall* presents special problems of interpretation regarding form and meaning. (p. 461)

Despite these multiple layers, the book's structure is anything but haphazard. Camus was a master of lucid, concise, carefully constructed prose, and *The Fall* exhibits all of these characteristics. The development of a form appropriate for his purpose is what is at stake in *The Fall*. 'For a man with a philosophical attitude to express and illustrate', Madden suggests, 'it would seem that the freedom of the essay-novel form is congenial. But to this freedom Camus has brought the artist's restraint and control' (p. 461).

The central character and narrator in *The Fall* is Jean-Baptiste Clamence. The book is structured into a series of sections the length of short chapters, but without chapter numbers. There is little in the way of a traditional 'plot'. Over a five-day period, Clamence addresses an unknown interlocutor in and nearby an Amsterdam bar, the *Mexico City*. His addressee never speaks, yet is always present. The interlocutor's actions and words, few as they are, are always only implied by what Clamence has to say. In his narrative, Clamence reflects on his own successes and shortcomings, and also makes pronouncements on a wide range of philosophical themes. We learn that he worked as a lawyer in Paris, but that he is now living in the Dutch capital and has come to describe himself as a 'judge-penitent'. He is currently middle aged, with a long history of triumphant cases and personal conquests behind him. Clamence's discourse with the unnamed, unseen bar companion traverses a diverse philosophical territory, addressing ontological, ethical, political, and aesthetic topics. He speaks of truth and justice, dishonesty and deceit, crime and punishment, status and hierarchies, freedom and slavery, memory and forgetfulness, courtesy, charm, love, friendship, death, faith, guilt, and judgement—among other things. He describes his relationships with women and with other professionals and intellectuals. He outlines some of his actions on behalf of others, both within and outside his profession. He discourses at length on his likes and dislikes, his whims and passions, and his superiority over others.

Described in these terms, it might seem as if the book lacks coherence and structure; as if it were merely a drunken rant. This is not so. Clamence's style of speaking is seemingly spontaneous, yet there is also a surprising deliberateness in his soliloquising. Indeed, there are moments of lucid sobriety in what might be expected to be a hazy, alcohol sodden environment. There is a progressive logic, without this seeming in any way contrived or mechanical, to the content of his narration, and as the monologue unfolds and Clamence peels away different layers of himself and his past, both the invisible partner in dialogue and the reader are taken in closer and closer. The forms of address to the interlocutor become successively more intimate, moving from the polite but anonymous '*monsieur*' at the beginning, to '*mon cher compatriote*', and finally to '*cher ami*'. In reducing the gap between protagonist and addressee in this manner, there is a corresponding reduction in what we might call moral distance. As Marcus (2006) observes, by emphasising the similarities between himself and the addressee, Clamence's account can be seen by the addressee 'not only as the story of another but also as his own, thus reinforcing his curiosity to continue listening' (p. 316). The ultimate addressee here is the *reader*. It is we readers who are invited in, who become not identical with Clamence but more understanding, perhaps more forgiving, of him. Clamence is *us*: not in the sense of standing for some universal 'type', but in displaying a kind of vulnerability that is shared by all, even if in very different ways. Clamence, by his own reckoning and as portrayed with artful skill by Camus, does not have a definitive 'essence' waiting to be found as the layers are peeled away; rather, if there is anything to be revealed, it is the importance of the act of revealing itself.

Camus went to some lengths to stress that he was not Clamence, asserting this in interviews and even including words to that effect on the back cover of one edition of the book (Todd, 2000a, p. xii). There are some obvious differences between the two men. Clamence is a bachelor; Camus was married. Clamence was not a member of the Resistance; Camus was. Clamence, having carved out his career in Paris, now resides in Amsterdam; Camus, while intimately familiar with Paris, spent only a few days in the Dutch city (p. xii). Yet, there are also similarities. Some of these are small details: Clamence loves sport and leaves his car doors unlocked, for example, as was the case with Camus (p. xii). At a deeper level, some shared psychological and personality traits can be identified: a certain self-assurance mixed with doubt, an easy charm around women, a sense of guilt for actions taken and not taken, a love of language, and a willingness to engage in the practice of self-criticism. There are other similarities: *The Fall* is, for both Clamence and Camus, a book about middle-age and the crises it brings. It is also a searching examination of the middle-class. When comparing the concentric canals of Amsterdam to the circles of hell, Clamence adds: 'The middle-class hell, of course, peopled with bad dreams' (Camus, 2000, p. 13). Clamence is not simply a self-portrait of Camus, but neither does he *escape* from his creator: Camus inhabits Clamence in subtle and not-so-subtle ways, infusing his character with aspects of his own experience, his thoughts and feelings, while also granting him the freedom to 'argue back' against those thoughts and feelings.

Those familiar with Dostoevsky's work will be struck by the parallels between *The Fall* and *Notes from Underground* (Dostoevsky, 1994a). Dostoevsky was one of the most important influences on Camus' work, a point that has been noted by a number of critics (e.g. Trahan, 1966; Wasiolek, 1977; Natov, 1981). Camus acknowledged his debt to the great Russian novelist in a number of his non-fiction writings. In *The Myth of Sisyphus* (Camus, 1991), for example, Camus makes reference to Ivan Karamazov from *The Brothers Karamazov* (Dostoevsky, 1991) and Kirilov from *The Possessed* (sometimes translated as *Demons*, Dostoevsky, 1994b) in addressing the theme of suicide. He also adapted the latter novel as a play. For Camus, Dostoevsky was a pivotal figure in contemplating the moral consequences of a Godless world. While Dostoevsky ultimately retained his Christian faith, he went to great lengths, particularly in *The Brothers Karamazov*, to consider contrary positions. It was Dostoevsky, together with Nietzsche, who prompted Camus and many others to ponder: if God is dead, does this mean all is permitted? Clamence encourages us to consider this question as well, albeit in a somewhat different way.

Both Clamence and Dostoevsky's Underground Man emerge as deeply complex moral beings. Clamence himself might argue against this, emphasising the apparent simplicity of his underlying impulses. He says at one point: 'I'd have given ten conversations with Einstein for a first meeting with a pretty chorus-girl' (Camus, 2000, p. 45). 'It's true', he concedes, 'that at the tenth meeting I was longing for Einstein or a serious book', and yet, he claims, 'I was never concerned with the major problems except in the intervals between my little excesses' (p. 45). Clamence confesses to many of his faults, yet also hides others, and through the very act of confessing displays certain virtues. By his own admission and account of his actions he reveals himself to be a deceptive and manipulative man. He is egotistical, hypocritical, insincere, and selfish; and yet he is not without some redeeming features. He is polite, charming, articulate, and refreshingly frank. He is an acute observer of the human condition. He has been very successful in his profession. He is as ruthless in deconstructing himself as he is in critiquing others. Clamence, in short, leaves the reader unsure of what to make of him. There is one crucial incident, however, that has a bearing on everything else. The consequences of this incident become clearer in the last part of the book, as the next section shows.

Vulnerability, Judgement and Confessional Pedagogy

Near the end of the novel, Clamence displays a vulnerability that has been largely pushed aside by his earlier boastfulness and confidence. This vulnerability is not completely disguised earlier in the novel. Readers learn, about midway through the book, that Clamence has been haunted by a single incident from his past. While walking to the Left Bank and his home via the Pont Royal in Paris one evening, in light rain, he passes behind a young woman leaning over the railing of a bridge and seeming to stare into the river below. He hesitates for a moment, but then goes on. After crossing the bridge he walks a further fifty yards or so and then hears the sound of a body striking the water:

> I stopped short but without turning round. Almost at once I heard a cry, repeated several times, which was going downstream; then it abruptly ceased. The silence that followed, as the night suddenly stood still, seemed interminable. I wanted to run and yet didn't move an inch. I was trembling, I believe from cold and shock. I told myself that I had to be quick and I felt an irresistible weakness steal over me. I have forgotten what I thought then. 'Too late, too far ...' or something of the sort. I was still listening as I stood motionless. Then, slowly, in the rain, I went away. I told no one. (pp. 52–53)

This event leaves its mark on the rest of the book. Clamence experiences what might be called moral dissonance, but underneath his overt charm and cynicism lies a seriousness, engendered by this one incident, he cannot hide. His efforts to cast himself as uncaring, frivolous, and lacking in conscience are never fully convincing, and in the last section of the book there is a marked shift in his tone and manner.

The last section is the only part of the book where the discussion takes place in Clamence's own home. Clamence is caught off-guard. His interlocutor turns up to find him, embarrassed, still in bed. 'It's nothing', Clamence offers, 'just a little fever that I'm treating with gin' (p. 88). The room is described as bare but clean. There are no books, Clamence having given up reading some time ago, disgusted with having a house full of half-read books. Having recovered his composure, Clamence recalls his wartime adventures, drawing attention in particular to his informal appointment to the role of 'Pope' among his comrades. His election was in response to the question: 'Who among us ... has the most failings?' (p. 92). Clamence, 'as a joke' raises his hand and is the only one to do so. Thus elected, he ends up taking the role seriously, discovering, with moral problems for which there is no simple answer, that it was not as easy as he had thought to be a Pope. As if to disrupt the reader's trust in him, Clamence declares his uncertainty as to whether he actually lived these events or merely dreamed them. Regardless, from the experience he takes one 'great idea': 'that one must forgive the Pope. To begin with, he needs it more than anyone else. Secondly, that's the only way to set oneself above him ...' (pp. 93–94).

After showing his companion a stolen painting he has in his possession (*The Just Judges*), Clamence approaches the climax of his five-day narration. This part of the novel is worth scrutinising in some detail. Clamence provides six reasons for not returning the painting, the last of which is that this allows everything to stay in harmony: justice is, once and for all, separated from innocence. This provides the basis for what Clamence now sees as his profession—that is, his vocation as a judge-penitent. His usual 'offices', he says, are at the *Mexico City*, but he practises well beyond this—'[e]ven in bed, even with a fever' (p. 96). Indeed, 'one doesn't practise this profession, one breathes it constantly' (p. 96). Clamence elaborates:

> Don't get the idea that I have talked to you at such length for five days just for the fun of it. No. I used to talk through my hat quite enough in the past. Now my words have a purpose. They have the purpose, obviously, of silencing the laughter, of avoiding judgement personally, though there is apparently no escape. Is not the great thing that stands in the way of our escaping it the fact that we are the first to condemn ourselves? Therefore it is essential to begin by extending the condemnation to all, without distinction, in order to thin it out at the start. (p. 96)

For Clamence, there should be '[n]o excuses ever, for anyone'. In philosophy as in politics, he says, 'I am for any theory that refuses to grant man innocence and for any practice that treats him as guilty' (pp. 96–97). Clamence is 'an enlightened advocate of slavery' (p. 97). Freedom, he has concluded, is too heavy a burden to bear. In a world where we are alone, without God, 'the weight of days is dreadful'

(p. 98) and for Clamence this means one must choose a master. Our moral philosophers, Clamence asserts, are hypocrites. They reject Christianity but, unable to stop themselves from passing judgement, take up moralising instead. They don't really want freedom or its judgements and, replacing Churches, they invent dreadful rules, avoiding the grace they truly seek—with its 'acceptance, surrender, happiness' (p. 99).

It was on the bridge that night in Paris that Clamence learned he too was afraid of freedom. We need masters, Clamence has come to believe, whoever they may be. It is essential 'to cease being free and to obey, in repentance, a greater rogue than oneself. When we are all guilty, that will be democracy' (p. 100). Giving away his own freedom, Clamence, through his work as a judge-penitent at the *Mexico City*, invites others to do the same. Noting, however, that his preferred solution of slavery is not immediately realisable, Clamence has had to find another means of extending judgement to everybody in order to make it weigh less heavily on his own shoulders. What he has discovered is this:

> Inasmuch as one couldn't condemn others without immediately judging oneself, one had to overwhelm oneself to have the right to judge others. Inasmuch as every judge some day ends up as a penitent, one has to travel the road in the opposite direction and practise the profession of penitent to be able to end up as a judge. (p. 101)

Clamence's approach to his profession of judge-penitent involves, first, 'indulging in public confession as often as possible. I accuse myself up hill and down dale'. (p. 102). This is not a crude exercise, but a process of skilful navigation, with distinctions and digressions as appropriate to each listener. Clamence goes further than this, mingling what concerns him with what concerns others, choosing features in common, experiences endured together, failings shared. 'With all that', he says, 'I construct a portrait which is the image of all and of no one', where people are led to wonder: 'Why, surely I've met him!' (p. 102). With the portrait complete, Clamence holds it out in great sorrow, declaring 'This, alas, is what I am!'. 'But at the same time the portrait I hold out to my contemporaries becomes a mirror' (p. 102). Clamence concludes:

> Covered with ashes, tearing my hair, my face scored by clawing, but with piercing eyes, I stand before all humanity recapitulating my shames without losing sight of the effect I am producing and saying: 'I was the lowest of the low'. Then imperceptibly I pass from the 'I' to the 'we'. When I get to 'This is what we are', the game is over and I can tell them off. I am like them, to be sure; we are in the soup together. However, I have a superiority in that I know it and this gives me the right to speak. You see the advantage, I am sure. The more I accuse myself, the more I have a right to judge you. Even better, I provoke you into judging yourself, and this relieves me of that much of the burden. (p. 103)

In this final section of the book, the interlocutor is also revealed more fully. Clamence sees him as 'a difficult client' (p. 103). Most of the others Clamence works with in his practice as a judge-penitent are more sentimental than intelligent. 'With the intelligent ones', he says, 'it takes time. It is enough to explain the method fully to them. They don't forget it; they reflect. Sooner or later, half as a game and half out of emotional upset, they give up and tell all' (p. 103). Clamence encourages his companion to revisit the *Mexico City* one day and to observe the details of his technique in action, promising: 'You will see me teaching them night after night that they are vile' (p. 104). In the last paragraph of the book, Clamence finally comes to the realisation that his interlocutor is, as he was, a lawyer practising in Paris. 'Are we not all alike', he asks, 'constantly talking and to no one, for ever up against the same questions although we know the answers in advance?' (p. 107). *The Fall* closes with these words:

> Then tell me, please, what happened to you one night on the quays of the Seine and how you managed never to risk your life. You yourself utter the words that for years have never ceased echoing through my nights and that I shall at last say through your mouth: 'O young woman, throw yourself into the water again so that I may a second time have the chance of saving both of us! A second time, eh, what a risky suggestion! Just suppose, *cher maître*, that we should be taken literally? We'd have to go through with it. Brr ... ! The water's so cold! But let's not worry! It's too late now. It'll always be too late. Fortunately! (pp. 107–108)

Literature, Philosophy and Reflection

By Clamence's own account, his work as a judge-penitent is pedagogical in nature: he is involved in teaching others to examine themselves critically. Like any other teacher, he has a range of methods at his disposal, but he adapts them to suit different people and contexts. His 'classroom' is the *Mexico City* and surrounding areas. Yet, this is by no means the only way in which the book can be read from an educational point of view. We can also ask 'What does Camus teach *us*?' and 'How does he do this?' What does the form of *The Fall* allow, from an educational point of view, that (say) a philosophy text might not?

Camus did not see *The Fall* as a work of philosophy, and were we to evaluate it in those terms, it would not be difficult to identify weaknesses. Key propositions, as enunciated by Clamence, are often left to stand on their own without robust philosophical argument. The ideas are not developed in a tight sequential, logical fashion. *The Fall* is aphoristic in its treatment of philosophical themes, recalling the style adopted most famously by Nietzsche in several of his major works. Clamence offers numerous brief, insightful remarks and observations and leaves it to readers to ponder their further significance. *The Fall* teaches through fostering a particular kind of reflection in those who engage the text. The novel is, as Brian Fitch (1995) points out, designed to *unsettle*—indeed, *disturb*—the reader. It is not, Fitch argues, a book one can simply lay down after having read it and walk away from; it has 'both an immediate and lasting impact upon its reader, who cannot emerge unscathed from the experience' (p. 120). 'It is not until its very last pages', Fitch adds, 'that the full import of its title is brought home to us and that we come to realize that its aim has been nothing less than to engineer the 'fall' of its reader' (p. 120). The reader, like Clamence's listeners in the *Mexico City*, becomes one of the judge-penitent's students. Camus thus teaches us to reconsider our own 'innocence'; to ask searching questions of ourselves as we sit in judgement of Clamence.

Of course, this kind of interrogation of ourselves is also possible through a standard work of philosophy. Strong arguments, with conclusions that follow logically from well-defended premises, can convince us to rethink fundamental ideas and, through this, to undergo a process of educational transformation. But the form of a work such as *The Fall* can have an important bearing on the extent to which, and the way in which, this process occurs. For *The Fall* is not merely about philosophical ideas in the abstract; it is about their embodiment in the life, words and actions of a central character, Jean-Baptiste Clamence. This allows us to see those ideas in a fresh light: to consider them in relation to their contexts (even if those contexts may be described in only vague terms in parts of the novel), and to recognise their imperfections, their tensions and contradictions, as well as their power and insight. They become not so much 'lived' ideas as 'live' ideas— subject to the ebb and flow of events, distractions and interruptions, questions and comments from others, the pull of strong emotions, and the shifting consciousness of the central character.

One of Camus' great achievements with the novel is to make it difficult for readers to 'pigeon hole' Clamence. Clamence is a complex character, but not in a contrived way. He is, as Nietzsche (1996) would have put it, 'human, all too human'. Throughout much of the book, he displays a certain self-assurance—an arrogance borne out of his success as a lawyer and the control he feels over others. He is open about his desire to dominate—his need to be 'above' others, even in a literal sense (preferring, for example, to be on the upper deck of boats and to take the bus instead of the underground). He notes that he never had difficulty in attracting women, and he outlines in some detail the ways in which he would manipulate his relationships with them. In the last part of the book, this veil of control begins to slip away, and Clamence, more 'exposed' at this point than at any other stage of the narrative, over-compensates. He lets himself get carried away by emotion, insisting, as if defending himself when no charge has yet been laid, 'I am happy, I tell you. I won't let you think I'm not happy, I am happy unto death!' (Camus, 2000, p. 105). He continues: 'I'm going back to bed; forgive me. I fear I got worked up; yet I'm not weeping' (p. 105).

Clamence has done much throughout the book to try and convince his interlocutor— and the reader—that he doesn't care for others, at least not in a genuine way. He notes early on that he liked to help blind people cross the street and defend 'widows and orphans' in court, but this, his narrative seems to suggest, is all for show. In the last section, with his guard beginning to fall down, he reasserts his selfishness. Just at the point where the reader might start believing his pedagogical work as a judge-penitent is more for the good of others than for himself, he says to his companion of the past five days: 'Admit ... that today you feel less pleased with yourself than you felt five days ago? Now I shall wait for you to write to me or to come back. For you will come back, I am sure! You'll find me unchanged. And why should I change, since I have found the happiness that suits me?' (p. 103). In case there was any doubt about his self-centredness, he adds: 'I haven't changed my way of life; I continue to love myself and to make use of others' (p. 104). Clamence, we might be quick to say, does not redeem himself; he remains egotistical, manipulative and hypocritical. In teaching others to examine themselves critically he seems to be driven less by a sense of care and respect for his learners, or for the good he might bring to their lives, than by the sense of personal satisfaction he gains from seeing people eventually break down and confess all.

Yet, the discomforting effect of Camus' work is that as readers reach the end of the book, the forms of judgement we might be tempted to pass on Clamence need, in turn, to be passed on us. We are all guilty, as Clamence says. Camus, through the character and words of Clamence, teaches us to reflect, but in the end we end up questioning not only ourselves—our motivations, our commitments, our relations with others—but the very process of reflection itself. As Solomon (2004) observes, Camus maintained an ambivalent attitude toward questions of innocence and reflection. His writings—not just *The Fall* but *The Outsider*, *The Myth of Sisyphus* and his lyrical essays and notebooks as well—encourage us to ask:

> How philosophical can one be without falling into the gloom to which philosophy is so prone? 'I tried philosophy', noted Doctor Johnson, 'but cheerfulness kept breaking out'. To what extent can one live the life of reflection which, contra Aristotle, both Kierkegaard and Dostoevsky likened to a kind of disease? Does reflection inevitably lead to a sense of one's own inadequacy? (Solomon, 2004, p. 52)

The notion of 'reflection' has occupied an important place in educational discourse over the years. The idea of a 'liberal education' is often promoted on the basis that it will encourage students to become reflective citizens; there has been a great deal of talk about the need to develop teachers who are 'reflective practitioners'; and reflection is a key element in the pedagogical theory of the influential Brazilian educationist, Paulo Freire. Many who address questions of spirituality in education also stress the value of reflection. *The Fall* unsettles us here: it prompts us to examine afresh our cherished assumptions about the worth of a reflective life. Yet in doing so, it provides tacit affirmation of the importance of reflection: it is, paradoxically, *through* reflection that we come to question the value of reflection. In both its form and its content, *The Fall*, once taken up by readers, becomes, as it were, complicit in this process.

Clamence himself is a reflective man, but only to a point. He seems to accept, if not relish, the fact that he forgets many things and that most events in his life leave few permanent marks on him. He undergoes a thorough process of confession, and encourages those he teaches through his role as judge-penitent to do likewise, yet his confession does not reveal all. We learn from Clamence's actions, from the *way* he talks, as much as from what he says. *The Fall* does not provide prominent signposts for the reader in this process, but subtle hints are there. The movements within and beyond the *Mexico City* earlier in the book; the shift in tone as

Clamence discusses the one event that seems to have left a lasting imprint on his moral life; and the more openly emotional quality of the narration in the last section: these all provide important contextual clues in deciding how to interpret the ideas presented to us.

The very fact that Clamence monopolises the conversation to such an extent—one commentator has called *The Fall* a 'dialogue of one' (Hartsock, 1961, p. 358)— tells us something significant about the relationship between the ideas and the man. Clamence, as we have seen, likes to dominate, to be in control. While implying that his teaching method involves listening as well as talking, we cannot know what this means in practice. Does he listen carefully to those he teaches when they reach the point of pouring their hearts out, displaying the patience his interlocutor has shown with his (Clamence's) confession over the past five days? At one point in the final section he seems to answer this question, saying 'I shall listen ... to your own confession with a great feeling of fraternity' (p. 103). But we cannot be sure what this will mean in practice, for the narrative finishes before we have time to find out. On the evidence presented in the text, Clamence seems to lack the kind of deep concern for the voice of 'the Other' that is often seen as necessary for authentic educational dialogue. This too, however, remains uncertain. With only one side of what could be a reciprocal conversational arrangement presented to us, and only Clamence's brief sketch of his pedagogical method to go by, there remains consider-able ambiguity about the form of dialogue being promoted.

Camus leaves no neat and easy 'answers' in *The Fall*. The value of Clamence's pedagogical approach as a judge-penitent remains unclear. We know that Clamence sees advantages in the process for himself—'I provoke you into judging yourself', he says, 'and this relieves me of that much of the burden' (p. 103)—but the question of whether reflection through confession is worthwhile for others finds no definitive resolution. Reflection certainly does not seem to lead unequivocally to happiness; if anything, there is greater emphasis on the sense of despair it may provoke. At most, Clamence seems to suggest, we develop a more honest under-standing of our shortcomings. 'Ah *mon cher*', he says to his companion, 'we are odd, wretched creatures and, if we merely look back over our lives, there's no lack of occasions to amaze and scandalize ourselves' (p. 103). Solomon (2004) suggests that Clamence and perhaps Camus may have indulged in the wrong kind of reflection, 'reflection that was already tainted with the other-worldly, with comparisons and contrasts to perfection, and consequently with the seeds of failure and resentment' (p. 53).

> This is the cost of what Nietzsche called the 'shadows of God': our continuing insistence to hold up superhuman ideals of perfection and then declare ourselves failures or frauds in their reflection. Thus the comparison and contrast with a perfect world makes this one seem 'absurd', and the comparison and contrast with either God or Christ or the *Übermensch* renders us pathetic, 'human-all-too-human'. (p. 53)

Solomon may be right in this assessment, but *The Fall* also calls these 'shadows of God' into question. Moreover, it is not merely the process of individual reflection that is at stake here, but the form of reflection established through a pedagogical relation. The reflection Clamence undergoes may not be the same as that experienced by his 'students', or, for that matter, by the reader. Nor should we take it for granted that despair is always ethically undesirable or to be avoided. (There is no suggestion here that Solomon assumes as much.) There may be educative value in the forms of despair promoted by Clamence's pedagogical method. Camus does not tell us the answer here, and we can only draw, at most, partial inferences about this from the 'results' presented to us by Jean-Baptiste Clamence. In the end, ambiguity and uncertainty prevail, but with them *possibilities* also emerge, and the reader is left to continue 'working' with the text long after the reading process has seemingly been completed.

Conclusion

Whatever our judgement of Camus as a philosopher, it is undeniable, I think, that works such as *The Fall* allow us to ponder important philosophical questions. *The Fall* provides a convincing demonstration of Camus' ability to bridge different genres of writing: to allow the literary to *become* philosophical via the forms of reflection engendered in the reader. Indeed, it can be claimed that *The Fall* transforms the reader-text relationship. This is the position taken by Brian Fitch (1995), who maintains that in *The Fall* Camus has developed a narrative form that is unique in the manner of its interaction with the reader. It is not simply a case of the reader becoming more like the novelist (as the French *Nouveau Roman* encouraged); rather, '*The Fall*'s reader becomes implicated in the reading on an existential level, as a human being with a past, present, and future that have nothing to do with aesthetics and everything to do with life as it is led' (p. 121). This chapter has concentrated on one aspect of life as it is led: the educational dimension, to which Camus, through the character and ideas of Jean-Baptiste Clamence, has something important to contribute. That readers at the end of the novel are left with further questions about exactly what this might be confirms rather than denies the value of the book. *The Fall* teaches us, whether we want to learn this or not, to continue the process of reflection already started by Clamence. This is, then, not a book one should pick up lightly: a decision to read *The Fall* is simultaneously a decision to risk upsetting and changing forever our view of ourselves, others and the nature of our ethical lives.

References

Camus, A. (1953) *The Rebel*, A. Bower, trans. (London, Hamish Hamilton).
Camus, A. (1960) *The Plague*, S. Gilbert, trans. (London, Penguin).
Camus, A. (1962) *Caligula and Three Other Plays* (New York, Vintage).
Camus, A. (1983) *The Outsider*, J. Laredo, trans. (London, Penguin).
Camus, A. (1991) *The Myth of Sisyphus and Other Essays*, J. O'Brien, trans. (New York, Vintage International).
Camus, A. (1996) *The First Man*, D. Hapgood, trans. (London, Penguin).
Camus, A. (2000) *The Fall*, J. O'Brien, trans. (London, Penguin).

Cruickshank, J. (1960) *Albert Camus and the Literature of Revolt* (New York, Oxford University Press).

Curzon-Hobson, A. (2003) Between Exile and the Kingdom: Albert Camus and empowering classroom relationships, *Educational Philosophy and Theory*, 35:4, pp. 367–380.

Denton, D. E. (1964) Albert Camus: Philosopher of moral concern, *Educational Theory*, 14, pp. 99–127.

Dostoevsky, F. (1991) *The Brothers Karamazov*, R. Pevear & L. Volokhonsky, trans. (New York, Vintage).

Dostoevsky, F. (1994a) *Notes from Underground*, R. Pevear & L. Volokhonsky, trans. (New York, Vintage).

Dostoevsky, F. (1994b) *Demons*, R. Pevear & L. Volokhonsky, trans. (New York, Vintage).

Fitch, B. T. (1995) *The Fall: A matter of guilt* (New York, Twayne Publishers).

Ford, R. (2004) Critiquing Desire: Philosophy, writing and terror, *Journal of Human Rights*, 3:1, pp. 85–98.

Gibbons, A. & Heraud, R. (2007) Creativity, Enterprise and the Absurd: Education and the Myth of Sisyphus—a challenge to an educator. Paper presented at the Philosophy of Education Society of Australasia conference, Wellington, 6–9 December.

Götz, I. L. (1987) Camus and the Art of Teaching, *Educational Theory*, 37:3, pp. 265–276.

Greene, M. (1973) *Teacher as Stranger* (Belmont, CA, Wadsworth).

Grobe, E. P. (1966) The Psychological Structure of Camus's *L'Hôte*, *French Review*, 40, pp. 357–62.

Hanna, T. (1958) *The Thought and Art of Albert Camus* (Chicago, Henry Regnery).

Hartstock, M. (1961) Camus' *The Fall*: Dialogue of one, *Modern Fiction Studies*, 7:4, pp. 357–364.

Hustis, H. (2007) Falling for Dante: The *Inferno* in Albert Camus's *La Chute*, *Mosaic*, 40:4, pp. 1–16.

Kaufmann, W. (1959) Existentialism and Death, *Chicago Review*, 13:2, pp. 75–93.

LeBlanc, J. R. (2004) *Ethics and Creativity in the Political Thought of Simone Weil and Albert Camus* (Lewiston, NY, The Edwin Mellen Press).

Locke, F. W. (1967) The Metamorphoses of Jean-Baptiste Clamence, *Symposium*, 21:4, pp. 306–315.

Madden, D. (1966) Ambiguity in Albert Camus' *The Fall*, *Modern Fiction Studies*, 12:4, pp. 461–472.

Marcus, A. (2006) Camus's *The Fall*: The dynamics of narrative unreliability, *Style*, 40:4, pp. 314–333.

Marshall, J. D. (2007a) Philosophy, Polemics, Education, *Studies in Philosophy and Education*, 26, pp. 97–109.

Marshall, J. D. (2007b) Philosophy as Literature, *Educational Philosophy and Theory*, 39:3, pp. 383–393.

Natov, N. (1981) Albert Camus' Attitude Towards Dostoevsky, *Revue de Litterature Compare*, 55:3/4, pp. 439–464.

Nietzsche, F. (1996) *Human, All Too Human*, R. J. Hollingdale, trans. (Cambridge, Cambridge University Press). (Original work published 1878.)

Oliver, T. (1973) Camus, Man, and Education, *Educational Theory*, 23:3, pp. 224–229.

Onimus, J. (1970) *Albert Camus and Christianity*, E. Parker, trans. (Dublin, Gill and Macmillan).

Orme, M. (2007) *The Development of Albert Camus's Concern for Social and Political Justice: 'Justice Pour Un Juste'* (Madison, WI, Fairleigh Dickinson University Press).

Sagi, A. (2002) *Albert Camus and the Philosophy of the Absurd*, B. Stein, trans. (Amsterdam, Rodopi).

Skrimshire, S. (2006) A Political Theology of the Absurd? Albert Camus and Simone Weil on social transformation, *Literature and Theology*, 20:3, pp. 286–300.

Solomon, R. C. (2004) Pathologies of pride in Camus's *The Fall*, *Philosophy and Literature*, 28, pp. 41–59.

Todd, O. (2000a) *Introduction*, in A. Camus *The Fall*, J. O'Brien, trans. (London, Penguin).

Todd, O. (2000b) *Albert Camus: A life*, B. Ivry, trans. (New York, Carroll & Graf).

Trahan, E. (1966) Clamence vs. Dostoevsky: An approach to *La Chute*, *Comparative Literature*, 18:4, pp. 337–350.

Vines, L. (2003) Kieslowski's *Red* and Camus's *The Fall*: Redemption of a judge-penitent, *Literature/Film Quarterly*, 31:2, pp. 141–147.

Vulor, E. C. (2000) *Colonial and Anti-Colonial Discourses: Albert Camus and Algeria* (Lanham, MD, University Press of America).

Wasiolek, E. (1977) Dostoevsky, Camus, and Faulkner: Transcendence and mutilation, *Philosophy and Literature*, 1:2, pp. 131–146.

Weddington, H. S. (2007) The Education of Sisyphus: Absurdity, educative transformation, and suicide, *Journal of Transformative Education*, 5:2, pp. 119–133.

Woolfolk, A. (1984) The Dangers of Engagement: Camus' political esthetics, *Mosaic*, 17:3, pp. 59–69.

5

Reading the Other: Ethics of encounter

Sarah Allen

> Then she opened up a book of poems/And handed it to me/Written by an
> Italian poet/From the thirteenth century./And every one of them words
> rang true/And glowed like burnin' coal/pourin' off of every page/Like it
> was written in my soul from me to you,/Tangled up in blue.
> —Bob Dylan, 'Tangled Up in Blue'

Most scholarly fields, at least in the humanities, have been asking the same questions about the politics of encounter for decades: Should we try to find a way to encounter an other without appropriating it, without imposing ourselves on it? Is encountering-without-appropriating even possible? Can we approach something in any way and know it for what it really is? Or, must we resort to thematization in order to encounter something or someone? In other words, can we encounter a thing without cognating it and thus committing an act of violence in gathering it to us, in making sense of it through a process of reflection that necessitates a return to me?[1]

Of course, these questions are profuse and taken up with intense interest in rhetoric and composition scholarship, as well as in literary scholarship. For example, much of rhetoric and composition scholarship addresses the question of encounter in discussions about our responsibilities as teachers: about how we engage and negotiate a variety of beliefs, values, and their inevitable conflicts in the classroom; about what texts we should use to present and discuss those beliefs, values, and conflicts; and about what writing-models we should introduce that best provide students with appropriate and challenging methods for re-engaging those beliefs, values, and conflicts. In addition, in rhetoric and composition scholarship and in literary scholarship, there is frequent discussion about which issues and texts should matter most precisely because of the beliefs, values, and conflicts at work in them.

These questions and discussions are bound up in one larger question: what are the ethics, which I loosely define as 'modes of encounter', of our work? *How* do we work, when we encounter others—e.g. texts, scholars, students, beliefs, values, conflicts? Surprisingly, though, this larger question is largely neglected in any discussion about how we—scholars of composition, rhetoric, and literature—should write.

In discussions about what and how our students should be taught to write, at least two genres of writing are advocated enthusiastically and often: the argument and the personal essay. Given the far more numerous textbooks on argument that are on the market, the former seems the more popular genre, particularly in composition classrooms. One might expect this of our pedagogical practices, of course, given the fact that the argument is the mode most often deployed in the academic article, in our own work. However, in the last 15 to 20 years, there has been a surge of interest in incorporating the personal essay into composition class-rooms and most recently even into our own scholarship.[2]

Perhaps unsurprisingly, there is quite a lot of tension between the two camps—mostly due to a concern about which genre is less tyrannizing and, as a con-sequence, more socially responsible. To put this in terms consistent with this chapter, much of the conversations I've read between those who privilege the personal essay and those who privilege the argument have hinged on questions of the ethics of encounter.

Specifically, the personal essay is critiqued for its enactment of the traditionally accepted relationship of the writer-represented-on-the-page. Thus, the writer's presence tyrannizes the page's content because (the assumption is that) the essay is necessarily the reflection of its author.[3] Consequently, the notable rhetoric and composition scholar, David Bartholomae, argues that students of what he calls ' "creative nonfiction" or "literary nonfiction" ' (1995, p. 68) write '... as though they [are] not the products of their time, politics and culture, as though they could be free, elegant, smart, independent, the owners of all that they saw' (p. 70).

In other words, the implications presented in Bartholomae's article, part of which is quoted above, are that the personal essay, as a subgenre of creative or literary nonfiction, allows for the perpetuation of the fallacy that a writer can be 'free' of social influences, 'independent' of a society and of its politics, and 'owners' of his/her own perspective and experiences—of those the writer expresses on the page, specifically. Consequently, if the writer is not conscious and critical of the social influences acting on him/her, if s/he believes the text to be the singular and uninfluenced production of his/her own self, then the topic taken up in the essay is tyrannized by the writer—is overridden, so to speak, by the all-consuming presence, which includes the relentless perspective, of the writer.

Of course, one of the complications of Bartholomae's condemnation of the belief that the essay works in a transparent relationship to its writer is that the academic article is also assumed to be in a direct (though not 'transparent') relationship to its writer, to be the product of its writer. Of the article and its writer, William Gass, renowned essayist and scholar of philosophy, states, '[An article] is a relatively recent invention, this result of scholarly diligence, and its appearance is proof of the presence, nearby, of the Professor, the way one might, perceiving a certain sort of speckled egg, infer that its mother was a certain sort of speckled bird' (1985, p. 26). This belief is so ingrained, in fact, that we, scholars of composition, rhetoric, and literature, use the author's name, when quoting a text. For example, see the last two quotes above that are introduced with 'Bartholomae argues ...' and 'William Gass states ... .' This practice suggests that I am not simply quoting the ideas articulated in an article but that I am quoting the ideas *of the writer* of an article.

According to Bartholomae, the writer of an article, however, is different from the writer of an essay because the former is one who is critical of his/her time, politics, and culture, or more generally, s/he is critical of the profound influences of time, politics, and culture on individuals. Thus, those influences, and the writer's unique perspective, cannot tyrannize the text, for the driving force in the text is not expression of the writer's perspective or the determining influences of the social forces at work on the writer. Rather, the text is driven by critique. Consequently, the article is not necessarily critiqued for its relation to its writer, like the essay is, for the writer of an article is, for example, 'diligent', to quote Gass, and 'critical,' to quote Bartholomae, i.e. the writer is rigorous in his/her engagement with, and critical of the social and political factors at work in, a text/issue.

Setting aside, for the moment, the snobbish inference at work in this description of the essay-versus-argument debate that the writer of an essay is somehow less diligent/rigorous, the genre of the argument admittedly has its problems, too. Typically, it is critiqued for brushing over ambiguities and complexities and for mowing down opposing views for the sake of establishing a new paradigm. Gass describes the 'look' of an article and its establishment of a new paradigm (i.e. its 'unassailable' argument) as such:

> As an article, it should be striking of course, important naturally, yet without possessing either grace or charm or elegance, since these qualities will interfere with the impression of seriousness which it wishes to maintain; rather its polish is like that of the scrubbed step; but it must appear complete and straightforward and footnoted and useful and certain and is very likely a veritable Michelin of misdirection; for the article pretends that everything is clear, that its argument is unassailable, that there are no soggy patches, no illicit inferences, no illegitimate connections ... . (1985, p. 25)

There are several issues that must be addressed in regards to the above quote from Gass's personal essay, 'Emerson and the Essay'. First, it should be noted that this critique of the argument is written in a personal essay—the genre generally butted up against the argument as its necessary nemesis, or to choose a kinder metaphor, as its 'tonic', as Chris Anderson argues in his well-known article on the essay, 'Hearsay Evidence and Second-Class Citizenship' (1988, p. 301). Yet, Gass (and Anderson) is doing the same thing the argument does: mowing down the opposition, or what I would call 'mud-slinging'. For example, neither scholar's engagement in the above passages is respectful of its 'opposition': Bartholomae claims that literary nonfiction allows students to falsely believe that they are not only free and independent (which are admittedly problematic), but also 'smart' and 'elegant'; Gass claims that the argument cannot possess 'grace or charm or elegance'.

Ideally, the personal essay, especially, need not resort to mud-slinging. It has its strengths in its privileging of skepticism, in its attention to complexity and complication, and yes, even in its existence-as-evidence of some quality of its writer. Also, very often an essay pays homage to works of other essayists, as in the case of Gass's 'Emerson and the Essay', instead of mowing down other works in order to establish its own reign. However, I show, using Gass's essay about Emerson's work, why the essay will continue to be devalued (in relation to the article) because of its reliance on and celebration of its transparent relationship to its author.

In general, essayists don't complain in their work about the belief in this transparent relationship; they advocate it. Thus, my purpose here is not to suggest that there is *no* relationship between the essayist and the essay. Rather, I will, in the latter half of this text, turn to the work of Emmanuel Levinas, which describes an approach to an other (writer/text) that does not hinge on the assumption that writer and text are in a transparent relationship to each other. I hope that in presenting this possibility for re-thinking the essay (and its relationship to its writer), writers, scholars, and teachers of the essay—and even its opposition—will give it new attention and explore further the possibilities that it may provide for engagement, for encounter.

Encountering in the Personal Essay

In 'Emerson and the Essay', William Gass employs the same literary form he is encountering in his scholarly (and personal) response to Emerson's work.[4] This employment is significant for two reasons. First, the personal essay privileges skepticism. For example, in his reading of Lukács theory of the personal essay, Robert Kauffman states that the personal essay 'comes closest to fulfilling its essential nature ... when it moves within a certain skepticism about its own presuppositions. Whatever conclusions it reaches must therefore be highly tentative in kind—temporary syntheses entertained by a mind ever ready to dissolve them so as to avoid reifying its own products and reflections' (1981, p. 89).[5] More precisely, the personal essay never reaches a definitive conclusion because to reach such a point would require submission to an end and to a certainty, both of which are antithetical to the work of the personal essay.

Instead, the personal essay works by unraveling presuppositions, which is not unlike the article; however, the personal essay is not interested in and does not work according to the movement of violent revolution. It does not dethrone, behead, and ascend the system of knowledge that it engages. If it did dethrone, it would have to set up a new reign, which would be like turning skepticism on its head and using it as the article does—as a strategy for establishing a new intellectual order.

This brings us to the second reason why Gass's deployment of the same literary form used by Emerson is significant: instead of 'setting up camp' and colonizing Emerson's work in constructing an argument about it—instead of standing on top of it and pronouncing Emerson's text's position in subordination to (i.e. serving simply as material for) Gass's reading of it—Gass is capable of a different kind of encounter.

The purpose of Gass's personal essay is not to appropriate Emerson's work, but to demonstrate the kind of work deployed in Emerson's personal essays—that is, both writers' essays explore (not argue) a concept. For Gass, the concept explored in his own essay is 'how is the figure of Emerson revived?' or, to put this in Emersonian terms, 'what is and how does one "to be"?'.

It seems that the work of the personal essay and the question Gass explores are irrevocably intertwined, so that in asking how Emerson is revived, Gass is simultaneously asking how the personal essay works. For Gass, the personal essay works by reviving its writer. This reviving is possible because in the production of writing and reading an essay, the essay restores the writer or event—the thing necessarily being written about—to life.

The Self Encountered in the Personal Essay

The process of reviving an essayist via his/her essay begins with a linguistic turn. After quoting a long passage from Emerson, Gass states, 'Emerson's mind and his imagination, the height of his royal aims, his loyalties, his hopes, the democratic cadence of his heart, are here. You or I read, and he is resurrected in that recitation' (1985, p. 15). To put this simply, resurrection happens through our reading the 'I' of Emerson's text. The reader is 'voicing' Emerson's 'I', his subjectivity—his position (and existence) as a subject. In this kind of encounter, the reader, literally, experiences the text-as-representation-of-its-writer.

This 'experiencing' not only happens because of a linguistic turn, but because, according to Gass (and many other personal essayists), the reader is allowed to see and hear the movement of Emerson's mind in an personal essay.[6] One sees it grappling with difficulties and complexities, and one experiences this 'grappling with' as s/he reads. As Gass says, '[A]s Emerson's mind moves from what is true ... to what is unlikely ... , we can *hear* how it happened' (p. 16, his emphasis).

We, readers of personal essays, are placed in a privileged position, where we have access to the vulnerabilities, uncertainties, and processes of skepticism at work in the mind of a writer, as it is represented on the page. As Lopate says, 'We learn the rhythm by which the personal essayist receives, digests, and spits out the world' (1994, xxvii). It may seem that this mode of engagement with an other is less totalizing, since it operates according to the preservation and resurrection of the other.

No doubt there is something wonder-full in this process, in a kind of reading that is interested not only in ideas and paradigms, but also in people. It is a dangerous kind of reading, as well, for in writing or reading 'about' people (even and especially an 'I') we are not as preserving and celebrating as we think. Rather, that preserving and celebrating comes at a cost, for one finds in such readings that the writer who speaks and is spoken is not 'safe', not impossible-to-be-imposed-upon. Rather, the possibilities for imposing paradigms propagate—for example, the paradigm of the writer represented (and thus capable of being studied/critiqued) on the page.

This is the strange contradiction in Gass's 'Emerson and the Essay'. Though writing a personal essay that, according to convention, should never arrive at any certainty, Gass is able to state with certainty what Emerson thinks and feels: '[Emerson] wished to become a Hero ...'; 'Emerson was obsessed with the problem of the Fall' (p. 17). As stated above, Gass believes we see 'Emerson's mind and his imagination ...' (p. 17) on the page, represented in the text and revived in reading. So the assumption seems to be that an attentive reader can interpret that representation (the writer), even conclusively. Thus, despite the fact that the personal essay does not say 'no' to the assertions of a text, it is not able to avoid totalization either. Gass's personal essay, specifically, totalizes because it assumes that an identity (e.g. Emerson) can be represented and appropriated to the text.

The Stakes

As stated earlier, Gass's equating the text to the writer is often the claim about subjectivity in the personal essay: the author is present on the page, or some version of the author is present on the page. This chapter, however, is not 'I' nor is any personal essay I write, for example. Black squiggles on a white page do not represent the essence of me (assuming there are such things as essences, of course). How could they? The process would have to operate along a line of abstractions that perhaps I am too ignorant to understand.

For example, how does this question represent me? In my experience, in the distance between myself and the keyboard, I and my gesture to connect or to convey become separate, though relational, things. I am not composed simply of a series of gestures, nor is the physical-body-me constituted by these words. This is a text, and it is presenting itself to you in your reading it. It may present one version of itself to you in this reading, but certainly that is not equal to one version of me.

When we assume that the text does represent a part of a person, we give ourselves permission to appropriate the text and the subject 'in' it. We necessarily do violence in such an encounter because we assume in those encounters that we can know the text, that we can thematize it, that we can summarize its main points and analyze its seemingly 'fixed' content, that we can and should perform an exegesis, because we are interested in getting the text right, in figuring out what it is about. Perhaps Gass is not interested in getting Emerson, the historical figure, right, but he is assuredly interested in the 'about'—for example, in getting the 'to be' right.

Gass states, 'Essays do not create—neither new worlds nor new philosophies. They are always written *about*; they are always either Of or On. On Reading, On patience, Of Friendship' (p. 30). To say that a text can be 'about' something—a topic, an issue, a question—is to assume a representational notion of the text. In other words, it assumes a kind of metaphysical relationship between the text and a topic, so that the one is a representation of the other, even if it is a representation of only *a part* of the other.

For example, the standard line is to say that *Moby Dick* is about a whale; however, the text is not a representation of a whale. It is, instead, producing a relationship between words and narratives and history (and whales) and on and on and on. Essays *do* create, as any text does, but when we talk of that production in terms of 'about' and 'representation,' it costs us the complexities and possibilities for other kinds of engagement. We are limited to exegesis, to 'getting it right,' instead of 'doing something with it'.

Though Gass's personal essay gets us involved by incorporating not only paradigms but also people, and though the text, at least at first, enacts an other-than-certain engagement with Emerson's work, ultimately it fails at avoiding certainty. Though the text is doing different work from the work of a traditional academic article—by demonstrating (instead of simply arguing) how language realizes an other—the text does so by performing an exegesis. This is because its metaquestion is 'what is Emerson and what is the essay about?'.

So, how can one respond to a text without appropriating it to oneself, without thematizing the content, and without setting up a new reign? Though Gass's personal essay does not work by setting up a new reign, it does take possession of the text, as Gass claims to find an Emerson in himself. It does so by thematizing— by asking what the text is about, concluding that it is about Emerson and about Emerson's 'to be' in essaying. The question becomes, then, 'How might we do something else?'.

Another Possibility

To begin, we must start with a different kind of question. Instead of asking, 'What is the text about?' we might ask, 'What work is it doing?' This means, then, that in our own readings of texts, we might, instead of listing the major problems of each claim in a text, begin by taking the work of the text very seriously, by saying 'yes' to its premises and claims, by asking what happens when one says 'yes': what are the stakes, the consequences, the necessities, the possibilities. In other words, instead of asking what is wrong with a concept or claim and arguing for why it is a problem, we might start by asking what it gets us—what relations, what processes, what questions, etc.

I do not advocate the 'art for art's sake' mentality here or mean to encourage reverence for the work that makes it god-like and unapproachable. Instead, I have two suggestions, both 'inspired' by Emmanuel Levinas's work: the first is a kind of 'homage-as-critique'. The homage-as-critique would work in several ways: first, it would privilege the encounter with the other in a way that at least *attempts* to avoid violence, that at least *attempts* a kind of welcoming, so that we do not meet an other (e.g. a theory, a text, a question, a claim) with the machete of traditional critique at the door, so to speak; second, the homage-as-critique makes us take seriously the merits of the work we are responding to, presents for the reader the merits of that work, and demonstrates how our own would be impossible without it; third, as such, the work stands on its own, as something we can work *with*, instead of functioning as the castle in the sandbox that we must smash to make our own.

For example, in his response to Buber in *Outside the Subject*, Levinas says something 'of the role [Buber] played by the very stature of his personhood and talent' (1993, p. 5). Thus, like Gass's interest in Emerson, Levinas is also interested in Buber-the-writer, and he too is able to assert certainties about the writer—about how Buber sees Judaism, what schools of thought he belongs to, and so on. But, this is interest-with-a-difference, for Levinas is not looking for Buber in a text. He does not simply thematize the character of Buber, or at the very least, he never assumes that he can know Buber, in his entirety, or even 'an' entirety. Instead, Levinas is interested in *Buber's work*, in what his work contributes to any part of Judaism, for example. To put it simply, when Levinas's work uses the word 'Buber,' it signifies not Buber-the-man but Buber's work.

Levinas spends the chapter presenting what work Buber has done, continuously reminding us that we are indebted to Buber for this work. At the end of the chapter, he does not come to a traditional critique of Buber's work but instead begins to address 'what Buber leaves us to ponder' (p. 19) in our encounter with the work. Thus, the set up in *Outside the Subject* is produced in order to push us forward from Buber's work, to explore other possibilities opened by the work. This is the form of the encounter deployed in Levinas's work. It begins with a set-up of an existing work, moving through some of the contributions of that work, all the while expressing gratitude for the steps made in those contributions to the development of philosophy, literature, Jewish thought, or perhaps even humankind, and then it explores possibilities for the 'where-to-now'.

That said, Levinas's encounter with Buber is not all niceties and acknowledgement, nor pleasant conversation. Often, the question that Levinas's encounter with a text prompts is the question that potentially unravels that text. But this is the point: there is something beyond the exegesis, beyond the understood, elucidated text. Levinas states, 'To conceive of the *otherwise than being* requires, perhaps, as much audacity as skepticism shows, when it does not hesitate to affirm the impossibility of statement while venturing to *realize* this impossibility by the very statement of this impossibility' (p. 7). Though much more complicated in the context from which this quote is drawn, here, it helps to demonstrate Levinas's project: to realize the impossibility of statement, while stating (affirming) that impossibility.

Thus, I will try to avoid any further exegesis of Levinas's text and instead discuss the engagement he enacts. Picking up where we left off earlier, then, Chapter 1 of *Outside the Subject* seems to be an *homage* to Buber's work. The work of the *homage* is significant and not simply because it demonstrates an interest in the writer-text relationship. For example, we've seen Gass's personal essay enact a kind of *homage* of Emerson's work in order to do several things: to set up the differences between the article and personal essay, to set up the significance of Emerson working 'to be', and quite simply, to set up the 'why' of Gass's choice to study Emerson's work particularly.

Like Gass's praise of Emerson, Levinas is equally interested in presenting the significance of Buber's work: to show where it differs from previous work, to show how it is significant to the question of encounter with the other, and to show, in turn, why he chooses to respond to Buber's work particularly. Thus, doing something with the work, other than dethroning and setting up a new reign, is imperative, but the *homage*-as-critique is only part of the work.

My second suggestion for a different, potentially less thematizing, mode of critique would be to take up some of the conversations in which the engaged work participates. Addressing how those conversations mold the work and it them, again, demonstrates a different kind of encounter—one which reveals what a particular kind of response to a particular conversation gets us. For example, Chapter 2 in *Outside the Subject* shifts from *homage* to a discussion of how ontology is influencing and is affected by Buber's (and Marcel's and Husserl's) work. This chapter is a much more thorough demonstration of how Buber's work participates in other, older conversations. Then, the chapter ends with a series of further questions that, in my own experience of reading, work to push the reader beyond the assertions of Buber's texts and into thinking of the *giving* of human beings differently.

Again, in Chapter 3 Levinas pays homage to Buber, reminding us continuously 'Nothing could limit the homage due him' (1993, p. 41). Then Levinas works, as he explains, to 'distinguish differences between Buber's positions and those I take up in my own personal essays' (p. 42). Thus, whatever critique Levinas commits is in the spirit of a kind of conversation, where he doesn't necessarily say where Buber's work is wrong and his is right but where his differs—how it responds to Buber's work.

Levinas states,

> Therefore in my remarks on Buber, though I indicate a few points of divergence, it is not to question the fundamental and admirable analyses of *I and Thou*, and even less to embark upon the perilous or ridiculous enterprise of 'improving' the teachings of an authentic creator. But the speculative landscape opened up by Buber is rich enough, and still new enough, to make possible certain perspectives of meaning that cannot always be seen, at the start at least, from the trails masterfully blazed by the pioneer. (1993, p. 42)

In other words, Levinas is not interested in showing how Buber's theory may be ill-informed. He's not interested, even, in arguing that interpretations of Buber's theory are ill-informed. Instead, he is interested in presenting other possibilities that were made possible in Buber's work. No doubt, Gass is doing the same in his work with Emerson's texts. Levinas, however, is much more careful in his work not to appropriate the work or to trample it, though of course some appropriation and trampling are inevitable (see his work on the *saying* and the *said*).

For example, after a discussion of how the approach to others works in Buber's theory, Levinas states, 'In my own analysis, the approach to others is not originally in my speaking out to the other, but in my responsibility for him or her' (pp. 43–44). He then elaborates on how 'responsibility' works. He never says anything about Buber's theory being mistaken or shortsighted or, even, problematic. Rather, Levinas plays it forward, turning out more possibilities, other possibilities, for negotiating 'the approach'. He would never say, as I've said here, 'Here are the problems with this work, and here's why we must seek out a better means'. Levinas is not interested in 'better'. His work is interested in 'the original ethical relation', which asks a far different question—what and how do we know?

Where to Now

So what does all of this mean for how we read a text? Taking our cue from Gass, first, we should try writing in other forms, forms that are not structured according to the maneuvers of the academic article. Levinas, too, writes in a different form, one that is different from the article. He begins with the homage; demonstrates some of the conversations the text responds to in order to encounter the work it has done; and then enacts a conversation between his own work and the text, which pushes the work beyond that which has been done, in order to ask other questions. These (the works of Gass and Levinas) are at least two possibilities, and to me, there seem to be many more.

Enacting a kind of conversation that does not say 'no' and does not so vigorously try to appropriate the text allows for a different kind of encounter. We may find in this kind of encounter, in the encounter that involves homage and conversation, not critique and tyranny, but work that acknowledges the impossibility of statement. It does not say, 'We know, and this is why.' Instead, it says, 'Here is a conversation that tends toward a purpose'. This conversation is not something we can recall in reflection, though. We must actually *participate* in a conversation, enact a meeting, approach, encounter. Exegesis is another thing, i.e. if we don't want the burden of priesthood, then perhaps attending to the approach of the other is a suitable option.

In Gass and Levinas's work, we see a couple of ways of negotiating that approach. The former works to preserve the other by celebrating it and works to appropriate that preservation to another task. The latter also celebrates the other, but not a thematized other. Instead, it works to affirm the impossibility of preserving or recalling an other. It says that we must celebrate the unthematizable other, that we must at least take a look at the conversations that may have enabled this particular 'other' response, and that we must, in our response to it, point to differences, not to right and wrong, for 'about' is not the question.

Notes

1. By 'return to me', in part I am referring to the practice of encountering, i.e. engaging and understanding, an other via one's own experience—or via what many of my students, friends, and colleagues commonly speak of as an individual's or society's unique 'perspective'.
2. See, for example, *College English* 65.3 (2003a) and 66.1 (2003b). The former is a special issue on Creative Nonfiction, and the latter is a special issue on The Personal in Academic Writing. Almost all of the articles in both issues argue for the incorporation of creative nonfiction/ personal writing in composition classrooms, and in the latter issue, Malinowitz's article laments the exclusion of the essay from her own work.
3. The author-as-reflected in the essay is a popular concept—so popular, in fact, that the essay is often celebrated for it (see Lopate, 1994; Sanders, 1991; and Hoagland, 1985 for example). Gass, too, will work from this premise in his engagement with Emerson's work, as will be demonstrated in this chapter.
4. William Gass's work, particularly this personal essay, has helped to lay the foundations for the recent thrust in composition studies to incorporate and valorize 'other' forms of engagement in scholarship and in the classroom. This personal essay is often cited in the works of Lynn Z. Bloom (1999), Wendell Harris (1996), and G. Douglas Atkins (1991), among other key figures in composition studies. The book from which the article came, *Habitations of the Word*, has received often complicated (because of an inability to pin down the work) but always reverent reviews (see Graeber, 1997; Dick, 1987; Cornispop, 1986; Shaffer, 1985; Kermode, 1985; Alter, 1985). In addition, Gass's interviews have recently been collected in *Conversations with William Gass* (University Press of Mississippi, 2003), and a special issue of *The Review of Contemporary Fiction* (Fall 1991) is devoted entirely to his work.
5. Georg Lukacs's 'On the Nature and Form of the Essay' (1974) emphasizes his theory of the form's epistemological skepticism.
6. See Hoagland, 1985, for a particularly explicit example.

References

Alter, R. (1985) Review of *Habitations of the Word*, by William H. Gass. *New Republic*, 192:10, p. 32.

Anderson, C. (1988) Hearsay Evidence and Second-Class Citizenship, *CE*, 50:3, pp. 300–308.

Atkins, G. D. (1991) In Other Words: Gardening for love: the work of the essayist, *Kenyon Review*, 13:1, pp. 56–69.

Atkins, G. D. (1994) Envisioning the Stranger's Heart, *CE*, 56:6, pp. 629–641.

Bartholomae, D. (1995) Writing with Teachers: A conversation with Peter Elbow, *CCC*, 46:1, pp. 62–71.

Bloom, L. Z. (1999) The Essay Canon, *CE*, 61:4, pp. 401–430.

College English (2003a) *Creative Nonfiction*, Special Issue, 65:3, (Jan. 2003), pp. 237–322.

College English (2003b) *The Personal in Academic Writing*, Special Issue, 66:1, (Sept. 2003), pp. 9–104.

Cornispop, M. (1986) Review of *Habitations of the Word*, by William H. Gass, *American Book Review*, 8:2, pp. 12–13.

Dick, B. F. (1987) Review of *Habitations of the Word*, by William H. Gass, *World Literature Today*, 61:1, p. 107.

Gass, W. (1985) *Habitations of the Word: Essays* (New York, Simon & Schuster, Inc.).

Gass, W. (Fall 1991) *Special Issue of Review of Contemporary Fiction*, 11:3.

Gass, W. (2003) *Conversations with William Gass*, T. Ammon, ed. (Jackson, MS, University Press of Mississippi).

Graeber, L. (1997) Review of *Habitations of the Word*, by William H. Gass, *New York Times Book Review*, 26 Oct., p. 56.

Harris, W. V. (1996) Reflections on the Peculiar Status of the Essay, *CE*, 58:8, pp. 934–953.

Hoagland, E. (1985) What I Think, What I Am, in: W. Smart (ed.), *Eight Modern Essayists* (4th edn.) (New York, St. Martin's Press), pp. 222–225.

Kauffman, R. L. (1981) The Theory of the Essay: Lukács, Adorno, and Benjamin, *Diss.* (San Diego, University of California).

Kermode, F. (1985) Adornment and Fantastication: Review of *Habitations of the Word*, by William H. Gass, *New York Times Book Review*, 10 March.

Levinas, E. (1993) *Outside the Subject*, M. B. Smith, trans. (London, Athlone Press).

Levinas, E. (1997) *Otherwise than Being: Or beyond essence*, A. Lingis, trans. (Pittsburg, Duquesne Up).

Lopate, P. (1994) Introduction. *The Art of the Personal Essay: An anthology from the classical era to the present* (NY, Doubleday), pp. xxiii–liv.

Lukacs, G. (1974) On the Nature and Form of the Essay, *Soul and Form*, Anna Bostock, trans. (Cambridge, MA, MIT Press), pp. 1–18.

Sanders, S. R. (1991) The Singular First Person, in his: *Secrets of the Universe: Scenes from the journey home* (Boston, Beacon Press), pp. 187–204.

Shaffer, B. W. (1985) Rev. of *Habitations of the Word*, by William H. Gass, *Journal of the Midwest MLA*, 18:2, pp. 29–34.

6

The Art of Language Teaching as Interdisciplinary Paradigm

THOMAS ERLING PETERSON

> The man who knows no foreign language knows nothing of his mother tongue.
>
> Goethe[1]

The Unity of Language and the Phases of Education

In this chapter I examine the art of language instruction as a paradigm applicable across the academic disciplines. 'Language' is understood broadly so as to encompass second languages, the languages of the arts and crafts, the notational systems of the sciences, and those of the experimental technologies. To learn a language one must absorb content on a variety of levels, from concrete to technical to abstract, and do so by integrating a variety of cognitive functions. To learn any language, including the languages of gestures, pictures and other signs, is to acquire another culture, to accept and employ a host of new gestalten which, as Goethe's aphorism suggests, alters one's vision of oneself.[2] Furthermore, to learn a language is to gain awareness of the nature of language *as such*. I suggest that this concept of language is lost on some educators who ignore the importance of the median or relational languages that connect the disciplines. As Ernst Cassirer writes, language is the essential tool that humans possess to negotiate common obstacles:

> There is such a thing as 'language,' something like the unity of the infinite variety of languages. This is decisive for me. It is for this reason that I start with the objectivity of symbolic forms because, with them, we possess in *fact* what, in thought, seems impossible. It is this which I call the 'world of the objective spirit. (Cassirer, 1970, p. 220)

With this notion of the objectivity of language in mind, one can assess the art of language instruction as a paradigm applicable across the disciplines. The radical novelty of Cassirer's assumption, backed up by his research into historical linguistics and the philosophy of symbolic forms, is that it declares the actuality of a median language that unifies the myriad languages of humanity. With this realization comes the vision of a language of learning that contributes to a communicative convergence between the arts and sciences.

The arts and sciences today are strange bedfellows. They are viewed as a kind of Hegelian polarity, symmetrical and oppositional, each possessing its balance of cognitive 'force'. But the metaphor of force and territoriality is outdated. If one considers the arts and sciences as a diversified whole comprised of elements imbricated in one another, then one might better conceive of a method of teaching the language of any disciplinary system as a manifestation of language as such. In reality, the qualified language teacher is always pursuing a language of relations, since he or she occupies a position both internal and external to the world of the expert or initiate.

In order to better understand the stages of learning a language, I cite Whitehead's three phases of education from his classic work *The Aims of Education*. The phases are cyclical and overlapping and depend for their effectiveness on a rhythm established by appropriate interchanges and borrowings. In Whitehead's conception the initial phase, of 'romance,' yields an idealized and mythic representation of life. In it the student experiences the beauty of nature and the nobility and oneness of humanity. We learn our first language in this protective climate and it is altogether appropriate to learn second languages in that way as well: as Whitehead makes clear the phase of romance does not terminate with youth. As Vico writes, 'There is no discipline which needs reason so much less and memory so much more than language ... . There is no other age better than childhood for learning languages' (1993, p. 135). The second phase, of 'precision,' is naturalistic in character and opens the classroom to narrative and the diverse perspectives of all persons involved. It yields detail and scope, and reveals the poverty of deterministic explanations of complex phenomena. Discipline and rigor are essential to this phase as the student learns the essential vocabulary and grammar of the field. In the third phase, of 'generalization' (or 'satisfaction'), one returns to the simplicity and elegance of the phase of romance, but, armed with the increased knowledge gained in the phase of precision, one develops judgment and ethical values. The three phases are consecutive and interpenetrating, allowing for the fact that students progress diversely in different disciplines. While language is the earliest of disciplines to be addressed—'The romantic stage of language begins in infancy with the acquisition of speech, so that it passes early towards a stage of precision' (Whitehead, 1929, p. 59)—the study of a second language typically comes much later, and thus serves as a case analogous to the sciences in which the romantic stage comes later in the life of the student. Even after the stage of romance is completed, romance continues as the 'background': 'It must be fostered for one reason, because romance is after all a necessary ingredient of that balanced wisdom which is the goal to be attained. But there is another reason: The organism will not absorb the fruits of the task unless its powers of apprehension are kept fresh by romance. The real point is to discover in practice that exact balance between freedom and discipline which will give the greatest rate of progress over the things to be known. [...] Furthermore, I hold that the only discipline, important for its own sake, is self-discipline, and that this can only be acquired by a wide use of freedom' (Whitehead, 1929, pp. 54–5). The art of teaching for Whitehead lies in the ability to blend the three stages, to possess 'rhythmic sway' (Whitehead, 1929, p. 54) as the learning proceeds.

As a foreign language educator, I can attest to the fact that each of these phases is present in the L2 (second language) classroom. Because of the multiplicity and variety of tasks undertaken in the language classroom, the need for mediation between levels and types of instruction is always a concern. Mediation is best achieved in an atmosphere of equanimity and support for dialogue. Such a milieu leads to the acceptance of risk taking, the promise of aesthetic enjoyment, and the expectation of intellectual growth. Teaching a foreign language involves experimentation and dramatization, choreography and spontaneity. It is useless to wrap the language lesson in grammatical rules unless those rules are enacted.[3] One such way is through the positive regression of role playing, an absorption in the phase of romance. By the same token, the phase of precision requires the memorizing of tables and tenses, rules (and exceptions), lists and catalogues. The language instructor is faced with a paradox: is language to be taught as a 'natural' phenomenon akin to L1 or as a 'cultural' set of matrices, in the manner of the traditional instruction of the dead languages, Latin and Greek? Veteran teachers know that neither option is appropriate, but that an integration of the spontaneous approach and that of rote learning can exploit the phase of romance in such a way as to optimize the phase of precision. This leads in time to the deeper, more intuitive phase of generalization in which 'the precise study of grammar and composition is discontinued, and the language study is confined to reading the literature with emphasized attention to its ideas and to the general history in which it is embedded' (Whitehead, 1929, p. 3).

Traditionalists in the field of language instruction rely on grammatical paradigms and rote procedures, batteries of exercises and tests. Orality as a key to literacy in L2 is not seriously considered. In contrast, many immersionists stress orality to a fault, exempting students from the onus of rigorous grammar tests. Being 'student centered', they frown on error correction and ignore the grammar-based techniques of the past. The divide between these poles is bridged by those communication-based teachers who combine the order of the traditionalists with the spontaneity and naturalness of the immersionists. One such teacher is Claire Kramsch, who has adopted the notion of 'third places' and 'third cultures' in order to refer to the 'boundary' between the 'culture ... of our past and that of our present,' she writes:

> ... we have to view the boundary not as an actual event but, rather, as a state of mind, as a positioning of the learner at the intersection of multiple social roles and individual choices. The stories of such border crossings and of the 'conversion' that leads a person to realize she is no longer the person she imagined herself to be are told over and over again by those who have lived them. (Kramsch, 1993, pp. 234–5)

Kramsch relates the experience of language acquisition to the recognition of cultural differences and the development of interculturality. By accessing popular cultures in the classroom, teachers and students can surmount the 'uncommon subordination and powerlessness' that accompanies the task of learning a foreign language. Third places are situations to be created in the classroom by means of a well organized yet spontaneous integration of 'instructional discourse'—such as grammatical and lexical lists, paradigms and drills—with 'transactional discourse' that deals with them in context, as cultural content and usage, and finally with 'interactional discourse,' including 'functional and situational role-play, simulation activities, and also stylistic exercises'. A third place is rich because it recognizes the fictional, ludic and artificial aspect of the classroom environment—neither first culture or second culture—as its own culture of becoming. Kramsch proposes a set of efficient and pragmatic tools so as to stop from stifling students of language and culture with overtly grammatical priorities:

> An educational philosophy that stresses only doing things with words runs the risk of helping maintain the social status quo; it has difficulty dealing with the teaching of culture, because cross-cultural competence, unlike pragmatic competence, is predicated on paradox and conflict and on often irreducible ways of viewing the world. (Kramsch, 1993, p. 240)

The progression in the classroom from an instructional to a transactional to an interactive language reflects the same ternary rhythm outlined above in Whitehead's three phases.

The Environment of Learning and the Literature Classroom

How the denial of third places is manifest in the institutional culture is apparent now as it was in 1925 when Whitehead wrote of 'two evils' concerning the 'training of professionals': 'one, the ignoration of the true relation of each organism to its environment; and the other, the habit of ignoring the intrinsic worth of the environment which must be allowed its weight in any consideration of final ends' (1925, p. 196). Whitehead insisted that the fields of knowledge a university student could be expected to cover were very limited; thus the number of academic subjects required in the undergraduate curriculum should be reduced to a number that suits the phase of generalization: 'When we have rid our minds of the idea that knowledge is to be exacted, there is no especial difficulty or expense involved in helping the growth of artistic enjoyment' (1929, p. 90). By reducing the number of specialized subjects, one promotes the acquisition of physical intimacy with working systems and languages. Howard Gardner has stated that today's students find themselves in a 'shopping mall of the disciplines' (Gardner, 1999, p. 54) asked to choose between increasingly narrow and professionalized fields; such an entrepreneurial approach to learning devalues third places and allows the arts to lapse amid the general neglect of the environment of learning.

Robert Scholes has written recently on the same matter: 'a few texts well-pondered may be more valuable than many texts consumed thoughtlessly [...] What we need is a greater variety of courses, with a constant and prevailing emphasis on the process of reading, along with whatever constraints on choices that a given faculty thinks appropriate for the best results' (Scholes, 1998, p. 39). Scholes defends the study of rhetoric and reading, which currently occupies a low rung on the teaching hierarchies. Concerning the 'how' of learning, Scholes suggests we discard outdated practices in the teaching of writing in the academic disciplines:

> For too long, we have designed curricula in order to do justice to what we perceived as our subject matter. What I am suggesting is that we stop thinking of ourselves as if we had a subject matter and start thinking of ourselves as having a discipline which we can offer our students as part of the cultural equipment that they are going to need when they leave us. (Scholes, 1998, pp. 36–38)

What is suggested by the above critiques is that a careful focus on language and reading in a broader range of courses, all of which focus on environmental awareness and the enjoyment of knowledge, could have a positive impact on the structure of curricula and degree programs. Scholes, for example, proposes that the current 'canon of texts' in the field of English be eschewed for the sake of a 'canon of methods' (pp. 105–9). Such would provide teachers with more direct interactions with students, who could be engaged analytically and in terms of their imagination as they experiment and test new hypotheses. To adopt such a canon of methods would require that educators be flexible and responsive to student needs, that they blend 'tight' or causal thinking with 'loose' or intuitive and inferential thinking.

Roland Barthes urged something similar, recommending that literature professors reorient themselves to their field so as to correct the pervasiveness there of 'tautology' and 'alienation.' Specifically, Barthes advocated the adoption of three principles:

> The first would be to reverse classico-centrism and to 'do' literary history *backwards*: instead of envisioning the history of literature from a pseudo-genetic point of view, we should make *ourselves* the center of this history. [...] Past literature would be dealt with through present-day disciplines, and even in present-day language. [...] Second principle: to substitute *text* for author, school, and movement. [...] The text must be treated not as a sacred object (object of a philology), but essentially as a space of language, as the site of an infinite number of digressions; [...] Finally [...] at every opportunity and at every moment to develop the polysemic reading of the text, to recognize finally the rights of polysemy, to construct a sort of polysemic criticism, to open the text to symbolism. (Barthes, 1989, pp. 22, 27–8).

Barthes' remarks reflect the stimulating atmosphere of the 1960s when semiology and related linguistic studies achieved wide intellectual currency. This sense of aperture and freedom reclaimed the validity of language and symbolism as against the 'pseudo-genetic' hierarchy that placed literature over language studies at that time. Such an opening frees one from the categories routinely used to classify authors, works, and genres, and enables one to propose new predicates of education. With the text construed as a 'space of language' one is free to reject the 'antinomy between literature as practice and literature as teaching' (p. 27). As

Barthes states, 'every reading derives from trans-individual forms: the associations engendered by the letter are always caught up (sampled and inserted) by certain codes, certain languages, certain lists of stereotypes. The most subjective reading imaginable is never anything but a game played according to certain rules. [...] There is no objective or subjective truth of reading, but only a *ludic* truth' (p. 31).

If one is to *play* with language one must know the rules! To construct a 'space of language' with the kind of freedom Barthes suggests requires the supportive climate of a dynamic classroom in which one's actions make a difference. As John Dewey wrote in *Democracy and Education*, the 'three R's' constitute an overly narrow pedagogical focus that ignores free choice and the ethical goals of a democracy: '[many educators] are aesthetic but not artistic, since their feelings and ideas are turned upon themselves, instead of being methods in acts which modify conditions' (1944, p. 135). The idea that language instruction is an art applicable across the disciplines is a profoundly humanistic idea. It implies a reinvestment in rhetoric and linguistic anthropology. The modern founder of this school of thought is Giambattista Vico, who argued for the symbolic and spontaneous view of language as a concrete manifestation of the spirit and affective intelligence. Not surprisingly, a commentator on Vico's educational philosophy has seen him as anticipating the ideas of Dewey: 'There could be no more explicit rejection of the adjustment theory of behaviorism; no more outspoken support, with two centuries of anti-cipation, of Dewey's conception of the dynamic process of learning' (E. Gianturco, in Vico, 1990, xliii). For Dewey feels there is an *'intellectual* factor in the more spontaneous play and work of individuals—the factor that alone is truly educative' (1991, p. 62).

Indeed, dynamically inclined teachers of language across the disciplines rec-ognize this educative faculty in the student and thus promote the corresponding activities. As Dewey writes: 'The natural or psychological activities, even when not consciously controlled by logical considerations, have their own intellectual function and integrity; conscious and deliberate skill in thinking, when it is achieved makes habitual or second nature' (1991, p. 62). Thus for Dewey, 'Discipline of mind is ... a result rather than a cause. [...] Discipline represents original native endowment turned, through gradual exercise, into effective power' (1991, p. 63).[4]

The Humanities and Cognitive Sciences

In his cogent analysis of the situation of education in the humanities today, Robert Proctor notes how classical studies have been eclipsed, leaving a void: 'Classical education may be dead, *but we have found nothing to replace it*'; and 'we must take the death of the Renaissance humanities seriously' (1998, pp. 143–4). He presents the pertinent works of Petrarch as they initiate and provide a point-of-reference to future humanists and educators. If for the great humanist Petrarch, 'the ultimate purpose of study was not to become learned but to become good,' in our day educators are '[obsessed] with technique,' so that, in the case of deconstructionism, one finds a 'total intellectual permissiveness,' 'a new kind of scholasticism' in pursuit of a career that is an end in itself: 'most of the current methodological fads in our universities today, such as quantitative analysis in the social sciences and the latest literary theories in the so-called 'humanities,' are of such limited application that having these techniques in one's head can often be an impediment to serious thinking' (pp. 147–8). Proctor critiques those administrator-managers who do not guide by moral example or aspire to virtue and wisdom. When colleges and universities fail to select administrators who are respected academics the space of learning is usurped by managers whose lack of preparation in the humanities leads them to avert any contact with the language and method of self-examination common to Cicero and Augustine, Petrarch and Goethe.

Proctor has asserted in his study of the humanities that for many academics, blinded by quantitative thinking and the preoccupation with technique, 'the past is dead'. Despite paying lip service to the humanities, such scholars view the human-ities from the perspective of an isolated personality or mind, an 'intensive self'. Such a view of the self sees knowledge as fragmentary and disconnected, adjectives that also describe many curricula and programs of study that have left behind the liberal arts tradition in favor of the 'utilitarian' and 'capitalist' traditions. Proctor writes, 'By looking carefully at how the Renaissance humanists read a modern self back into the ancients, we discover another kind of self, the ancient extensive self, with its ideal not of autonomy and radical freedom, but of harmony and unity with the whole world of being' (pp. 173–4).[5] Denouncing the 'great collective amnesia' occasioned by the 'death of the past' in our universities, Proctor urges the imple-mentation of an aggressive and integrated four-year undergraduate liberal arts curriculum that will reestablish the sense of wholeness, of human connectedness with the cosmos through history, and the practice of contemplation of the divine. Such a curriculum can be applied to science majors as well as humanities majors and will require the student to ask the larger and more general questions concern-ing one's place in the world. Proctor treats the Renaissance as a kind of hinge or point of arrival of the ancient world. At the genesis of this rebirth is Petrarch, who provides a model of dynamic self-inquiry and a critique of scholasticism and its detriment of the life of the soul. Indeed Petrarch serves as a model for teachers of any era who seek a common language of learning. Without such a language one cannot ask those questions that guarantee the rigor and validity of the disciplines by contextualizing them holistically.

To engage in self-inquiry, therefore, is to espouse the 'ancient extensive self' that sees the individual as part of a cosmic whole; it is also to partake of the unity of all language enunciated by Cassirer. It is also to endorse the cited view of White-head that the only proper discipline in education is self-discipline; and it supports the idea expressed in the title of Hans-Georg Gadamer's 'Education is Self-Education,' where the philosopher emphasizes foreign language learning as an intrinsic com-ponent of self-education. Gadamer urges that language educators not adopt the traditional reading-oriented approach to L2, but promote active conversation: 'I am firmly convinced of this point: that far too often we view the learning of foreign languages as a one-sided relationship and not as an understanding of each other. [...] The most important feature in my own view is to be able to answer when one is asked, to be able to formulate questions oneself and to be able to accept corresponding answers' (2001, p. 533).

A major obstacle to such a view of self-inquiry is the territorial representation of knowledge referred to above. Curriculums are devised that leave students little choice; courses involving creativity are distinguished from those demanding intellectual rigor. While students cover the basic areas with stadium-style introductory courses, these courses do little to teach them about what is good, true or beautiful. Subliminally, students are taught that professors haven't the time to scrutinize their writing and that good test-taking skills are the key to success. What is lost in the process are the linguistic abilities that are the claimed goals of coverage requirements: flexibility, adaptability, the communication of relational knowledge. These are lost because students are not asked to blend concrete, abstract and technical skills in a dynamic and non-trivial way. The stadium classes tend to rely on rote instruction. Tests are often not returned to students and can be the sole source of one's final grade. Viewed in terms of the art of language instruction, such practices and curricular patterns tend to trivialize the radical novelty of L2's emergence in the subject's life and thus the adventure of language. The cybernetic alternative ('cyber-' from Greek, *kybernan* to steer, govern) to such a course is an educational dialogue in which the teacher uses the multiple languages of the discipline to direct and orient, to steer and constrain the students, so as to engage them in a learning conversation.

As Heinz von Foerster alleges, we are suffering as a society from an epidemic of perceptual disorder, in particular as regards our perception of the *future*; he argues that the one 'common denominator that would identify the root of the entire syndrome' is the tendency to only ask trivial questions, and the tendency 'if we encounter non-trivial machines, to convert them into trivial machines,' (where the term machine 'refers to well-defined functional properties of an abstract entity') (1984, pp. 201–02):

> Wouldn't it be fascinating to contemplate an educational system that would ask of its students to answer 'legitimate questions' that is questions to which the answers are unknown. Would it not be even more fascinating to conceive of a society that would establish such an educational system? (1984, p. 203)

It takes courage to affirm that information is not a commodity but the sign of a relation; that knowledge is not information but the awareness of a cognitive difference that begets complexity; that wisdom is not knowledge but a simplicity that stands above complexity; and that the two-pronged approach of a strict specialization shored up by area requirements is obsolete.[6] When such an archaic model persists, student choice is restricted and the work ethic imparted has little to do with individual motivation or the challenge to be an ethical person. When L2 is brought under the control of L1, one remains essentially monolingual. One is acculturated without being asked to define for oneself what one's culture genuinely is. Educational culture is all around one in the academy, and yet it is hidden; to seek out this culture the younger educators must inquire of their mentors. It is often only in speaking that the unwritten lore and practice of the older members of the profession is revealed.[7] What these masters tell us is that to gain competency in a new language generates satisfaction about something one has made. Such an experience is discouraged by programs in which the student does not actively apply the knowledge he or she has acquired.[8]

Classroom Narratives and the Convergence of Knowledge

One of the most effective means of enacting one's linguistic knowledge is narrative. As Galal Walker and Mari Noda write concerning the use of narrative in the foreign language classroom:

> The flow of social life occurs in a sequence of *performances*; discrete frames of specified times, places, roles, scripts, and audiences [...] The implications of this concept of performed culture for language study is that no one really learns a foreign language. Rather, we learn how to do particular things in a foreign language; and the more things we learn to do, the more expert we are in that language. (Walker & Noda, 2000, pp. 189–90)

The authors conclude, 'The question confronting those of us in foreign language study is, Which culture is associated with the language being taught in the foreign language classroom—the target culture or the base culture of the student?' (p. 190). Too often, the 'saga' that is repeated in the classroom finds the teacher playing the part of the teacher and the student playing the part of the student. But if one resists, one may bring the performative function into focus, and along with it the world of will. The defense reaction of students and teachers is to act out their lowest expectations and not to aspire to change what they assume they cannot. What does work are stories that students can enter into and assimilate, scenarios they can imagine. Role-playing means accessing the imagination, inventing situations and not accepting those already formulated. It means using ambiguity and taking risks, as occurs in the world when two people combine their partial knowledges of a subject to form a greater knowledge. The language teacher's use of dramatistic, performative and narrative modalities for the sake of opening up the classroom to uncertainty, risk-taking and adventure, has the additional effect of training students to respond to contingencies. This is applicable to the languages of other disciplines as well. Whether in the humanities, the social and human sciences, information technologies, or hard sciences, the use of role-playing (e.g. in the formation of hypotheses) allows students to appropriate the disciplinary language in a non-trivial way and transform the data of scientific experimentation into actual knowledge. If the teacher is successful in stimulating such activity, it will be an art, since a still coarse instrument is being used to cultivate observation, reflection and contemplation of knowledge.

Language teachers know that language learning is doubly rewarding: to begin with, one learns to communicate in L2. But just as remarkable is the change that comes about in one's person: as one appropriates L2, one gains objectivity toward

L1. This change provides the subject with positive feedback about the transformative nature of language itself. The complexity and subtlety of language resides in the fact that it is both product and event, code and utterance, *langue* and *parole*: language is something made and something that happens. In language teaching this duality is often communicated by means of analogy: for example, a teacher may start with lists of cognates between L1 and L2, revealing a taxonomy of pre-possessed knowledge of L2; as students experience more and more patterns and strings of language, they can perform more tasks in L2; in this process the language that was consciously *made* becomes the language that simply *happens*. The habits that attach to linguistic identity loosen and, as a result, one learns better how to learn. The student is constantly receiving new information and translating it into the language of the already known; the process can be thought of in terms of an ascending spiral as linguistic tasks are 'hard wired' so as to eventually become second nature.

Consider, for example, the ear's ability to sort through speech in which there are no pauses between words, in order to intuit where one word ends and another begins. This mechanism operates universally in children and adults alike, as the auditory intelligence parses the rhythms of speech according to predictable patterns, benefiting from constant exposure, systematic repetition and recitation of ever-longer units of speech. Recent research has shown the unconscious nature of this assimilation of auditory patterns. Rhythm is critical, since our bodies and sensoria assimilate patterns only through repetition and conditioning, which 'wiring' in L2 prepares us to improvise, to create, to converse. Through rapid transitions and recombinations of examples from the multiple strata of the language paradigm one can achieve syntheses that blend clarity and complexity. This 'division of labor' in the sensory reception of language would seem to confirm another insight of Whitehead's: 'It is a profoundly erroneous truism, repeated by all copy books and by eminent people when they are making speeches, that we should cultivate the habit of thinking of what we are doing. The precise opposite is the case. Civilization advances by extending the number of operations which can be performed without thinking about them' (1958, pp. 41–42).

There are fundamental differences between the languages of the humanities and the sciences, but there is also a deep commonality. For scientists as for humanists the rhythms of education and deutero-learning focus on actuality and narrative, becoming and perishing, environmental awareness and the pursuit of reasonableness. Clearly the sciences are based on the amassing of general rules or laws based on the rational conclusions that are drawn from controlled experiments repeatable by other experimenters at other times; it is easy to juxtapose the metaphorical procedure of literary minds and artists to this procedure and to conclude that scientists and humanists are worlds apart. But such would be to confuse the techniques of particular *metiers* with the broader conception of knowledge that is the goal of a liberal arts education. It is only in the neglect of this goal that some scientists feel compelled to extricate facts from values. As Stephen Toulmin writes: 'In the Academy, human scientists as much as natural scientists are expected to treat the contrast between facts and values not just as a distinction, but as a downright separation. Yet how can we do factual work in our scientific theorizing, while recognizing "values" in all our practical activities and relations?' (2001, p. 45) This syndrome has led to a compartmentalization of the disciplines that confuses rationalism for reason. As Edgar Morin writes concerning the need to reform the academy: 'Tremendous obstacles that hinder the exercise of pertinent knowledge have accumulated right within our education systems. These systems make the disjunction between the humanities and the sciences, and the division of the sciences into disciplines that have become hyper-specialized, self-enclosed' (Morin, 2001, p. 33). The nature of these obstacles is linguistic and concerns the failure to formulate a language of relations.

Lynn Margulis, the ecologist known for her explication of the Gaia hypothesis, has written a series of books about speciation, genomes and 'symbiogenesis,' defined as 'the origin of new tissues, organs, organisms—even species—by establishment of long-term permanent symbiosis' (1998, p. 6). An important concept that emerges in her studies is anastomosis, the union of parts or branches—as of streams, blood vessels, or leaf veins—so as to intercommunicate: 'Biologists call the coming together of branches—whether blood vessels, roots, or fungal threads—anastomosis. Anastomosis, branches forming sets, is a wonderfully onomatopoetic word. One can hear the fusing' (p. 52). Models of convergence such as symbiogenesis and anastomosis are vital in allowing scholars to negotiate and compare the diverse languages and logical fields of their specializations. How the languages and codes of the disciplines interrelate is analogous to how the individual learner absorbs and organizes data and conflicting hypotheses in order to construct knowledge. Mary Catherine Bateson, has written: 'The Gaia hypothesis pulls the data together, but it goes further by offering a metaphor for organizing awareness of the interconnections. Beyond that, it proposes empathy as a way of knowing and imagining connections about which we cannot yet be explicit' (1991, p. 140). Empathy or the language of the heart is a means of confirming the importance of the indefinite; while the experimental sciences usually gauge success by the predictability and repeatability of results, in today's global community the pragmatic realities of life are often pervaded by uncertainty and vagueness. It is so in the world at large but also in the relationships developed within the academy. As scholars confront unique and concrete situations, language itself evolves in ways that are unpredictable.

Unpredictability is a common problem to the arts and sciences, negotiated diversely and with contrasting methodologies; by the same token, predictability and convergence of systems is a shared epistemological and pedagogical goal. Because of this, communciation studies about the systematic means available to identify such processes of differentiation and analogy are necessary skills to the scholar. In his chapter 'Convergence of Science and Psychiatry' (in Bateson & Ruesch, 1951, pp. 267–75), Gregory Bateson predicts a convergence between these fields based on shared emerging trends, which include a focus on larger gestalts, on group interactions, and on relativist over absolutist approaches to knowledge, and thus on a less quantitative attitude taken toward the nature of experimental variables. As sciences benefit from research in psychiatry and alter their narrow, quantity-based self-definitions, and as psychiatry becomes a more interactive and humanistically informed field of study, the humanities too benefit. As Peter Harries-Jones has written, summarizing Gregory Bateson's notion of co-evolutionary processes:

> Predictable processes are *convergent* processes. Convergent processes are contrasted with divergent processes, processes which in time can never be predicted. Thus the relation epigenesis/tautology can be compared with the relation somatic adjustment/learning; as convergent processes, they can be contrasted with their opposite, divergent processes. (Harries-Jones, 1995, p. 253)

Some scholars have paid the price for pursuing such convergences between fields of knowledge in a scientific community unreceptive to nonconformists. Candace Pert is a neurochemist who has specialized in receptors, making a fundamental discovery concerning opiate receptors. She continued her NIH-sponsored research on neuropeptides (which constitute the vast majority of the 'ligands' that attach to receptors, inducing change in the cellular structure—along with neurotransmitters and steroids) by becoming an authority on the importance of emotion in neuro-chemical process. Pert explores the boundary between the conscious and uncon-scious 'bodymind': 'It could be said,' she writes, 'that intelligence is located not only in the brain but in cells that are distributed throughout the body, and that the traditional separation of mental processes, including emotions, from the body is no longer valid' (Pert, 1997, p. 187). One sees in Pert's initiatives (and those of likeminded scientists) an awareness of the associational nature of mind and a dedication to reformulating the scientific language of neurochemical processes to account for observable convergences of somatic processes and learning. Pert's research extends into the area of learning and the proper reformulation of the language of learning adopted by scientific educators in order to acknowledge the current change in paradigms; thus one thinks of her consonance with the scientists, humanistic thinkers and language educators cited above: Weiner, Scholes, Barthes, Kramsch, Whitehead. Pert is inspired by Gregory Bateson and shares his estimation of the importance of information theory in the recasting of our views about health and sickness, and about the curing role of the physician and the abilities that patients under the proper guidance can possess to insure their own good health and happiness. Pert battled with the NIH grant establishment and lost, in particular as regards work on one ligand, 'Peptide T,' as an AIDS treatment. She also worked with her husband Michael Ruff on early cancer research in the emerging field of psychoneuroimmunology (which they call psychoimmunoendocrinology). For our purposes it is critical to note Pert's insistence that interdisciplinary work in the biological sciences, along with the change in the language of research and teaching to allow for the 'bodywide communication system,' has emerged as a new paradigm replacing the 'old paradigm insistence on the separateness and autonomy of the individual disciplines' (Pert, 1997, p. 174). The thinking and decision-making that should be at the heart of higher education is compromised when, disengaged from creativity and risk, the scholar is limited to a narrow specialization or a diluted interdisciplinarity.[9] As all good teachers know, successful teaching depends on students who choose to learn. When language loses its vibrancy and student choice is diminished for the sake of a standardized final product, one loses the lesson of empathy.

Another positive instance of the phenomenon of convergence in scientific language is found in strategic psychotherapy, a discipline which takes a stand against traditional psychotherapy, asking the therapist to get involved with the patient and not be a detached authority figure. This is not to deny the professional know-how of the therapist, but to deemphasize the hieratic position of the expert who examines the patient, identifies the malady, and attempts to induce proper actions by changing misshapen ideas. The strategic therapist enters *into* the problem, which is conceived as something that concerns all those the patient comes into contact with. The initial definition of the problem is essential and must not be rushed. Steps and procedures must be selected in the proper sequence and at the proper levels of difficulty and must be gauged according to the situation, not repeated from a pre-established list. A small positive change should not go unacknowledged. The patient's expectations should guide the therapy since the very act of formulating expectations effects change. By being a good listener so as to ensure the involvement of 'other' and 'world' in the therapeutic context, the therapist can respond to symptoms reported by the patient. To summarize, the strategic therapist engages in four 'heresies': Choose Probability over 'Truth', Focus on How Rather Than Why, The Therapist is Responsible, and Change Comes *Before* Insight (Nardone & Watzlawick, 1993, pp. 17, 20, 22, 28).

It is apparent that these four premises also apply to the teachers of language. Language teachers eschew abstract versions of the truth, favoring the probable; they assume responsibility for learning and look for how, not why it is accomplished. In language teaching one discovers that the ability to produce in L2 is preceded by comprehension, an activity which is silent but not passive. Effective teachers invent activities that put language to use in rhythmic sequences and not as isolated, trivial, data; such interactive work also benefits the group dynamic and *esprit de corps*. The student is a collaborator whose creative imagination depends on the integration of mechanisms and sensations that converge toward the production of a work. This is part of the 'how' of change: it involves constant, direct exposure to the materials of the language—letters, sounds, words—as teachers create concrete and technical exercises that allow the language to emerge in its own inherent rhythms.

This notion of group activity and improvisation was highly regarded by Gadamer, who in highlighting the critical importance of foreign language instruction focused on phonetics and the accurate sounding of the language so as to promote conversations. Just as the acquisition of L1 depends on game-playing and ongoing experimentation, so do the learning of L2, and the maturation of the *forma mentis* generally. In Gadamer's view, one cannot separate out the learning of languages from the overall Bildung or cultural formation of the individual. This is a process that depends on the mystery and strangeness, the 'alien' nature, of L2. It is this sense of otherness that motivates one in a social setting to mimic L2 so as to appropriate it and penetrate its sense of otherness. As Gadamer writes: 'To seek one's own in the alien, to become at home in it, is the basic movement of spirit, whose being is only return to itself from what is other. Hence all theoretical Bildung, even the acquisition of foreign languages and conceptual worlds, is merely the continuation of a process of Bildung which begins much earlier. Every single individual who raises himself out of his natural being to the spiritual finds in the language, customs and institutions of his people a pre-given body of material which, as in learning to speak, he has to make his own' (1975, p. 15). Gadamer's remarks confirm—in the spirit of Goethe's aphorism cited as our epigraph—that the state of alienation is inevitable until the individual confronts it by learning another language.

It was in pursuit of similar humanistic goals, including the training in a median language of scholarship, that Whitehead and three other colleagues formed at Harvard, in 1931, the Society of Fellows. The objectives of the Society were stated as being comparable to those of Trinity College in England:

> Not the all-round man but the man who can open new paths is particularly wanted. Lines of work between disciplines today well established are the most promising for tomorrow's investigation. As Whitehead pointed out, new advances are made by working within present experimental error. The conventional fields are blanketed by fellowships that take better care than the Society can of the man who should get right to work on his final job. (Brinton, 1959, p. 25)

Even the most gifted candidates, if disinclined to invention and experimentation, were not appropriate fellows. The rarer 'geniuses,' more vulnerable to the institutional categories of the University, were favored, because better prepared to cross-pollinate—to converge—with the ideas of other fellows. A comprehension of this creative process requires that one have the ability to recognize the events and relations that foster it. The Society was formed as a means of establishing an antidote to the strictures of the departmental system. Diametrically opposite such efforts as those to recast the German University in an authoritarian and Fichtean mold, the Society fostered the growth of such figures as Robert Lowell, W. V. Quine, B. F. Skinner, Renato Poggioli, Allen Mandelbaum and Martha Nussbaum, intellectuals who outgrew the parameters of the departments and saw the traditionalist-progressivist gloss on educational techniques as a cliché. In the colloquy at Harvard one found the true glow of the humanities. Key aspects of this ongoing program are the freedom given the Fellows to do research unimpeded by formal requirements, the informal and convivial sharing of their work, and the concern for knowledge at the boundaries of current disciplines. It was the idea of the Society of Fellows that each individual has a discrete potential. Thus it '[encouraged] the development of each man (*sic*) in his own way, toward his own personal and independent achievement, as the result of his own private initiative. To establish such a condition in an American college would be to work a revolution.' (Brinton, 1959, p. 49).

A critical issue in this regard is the training of teachers. Graduate students are the future professors, but is it advantageous to assign them heavy teaching loads while they are still completing their coursework? Are admissions standards actually lowered in some cases to enable large departments to increase their number of low paid teachers? Scholes has advocated a reduction in the number of graduate students in the humanities and a dramatic increase in the years of commitment a university offers the candidate in support and training, so as to allow future educators to hone the craft of teaching as well as the scholarly treatise. This idea is not new. In 1950 Norbert Weiner argued for making the PhD dissertation a more challenging and decisive intellectual step forward and culmination in the student's life:

> In view of this great bulk of semi-mature apprentices who are being put on the market, the problem of giving them some colorable material to work on has assumed an overwhelming importance. Theoretically they should find their own material, but the big business of modern advanced education cannot be operated under this relatively low pressure. Thus the earlier stages of creative work, whether in the arts or in the sciences, which should properly be governed by a great desire on the part of the students to create something and to communicate it to the world at large, are now subject instead to the formal requirements of finding PhD theses or similar apprentice media. (Weiner, 1950, p. 133)

The great cybernetician adds in conclusion a personal note:

> What sometimes enrages me and always disappoints and grieves me is the preference of great schools of learning for the derivative as opposed to the original, for the conventional and thin which can be duplicated in many copies rather than the new and powerful, and for arid correctness and limitation of scope and method rather than for universal newness and beauty, wherever it may be seen. (Weiner, 1950, p. 135)

It would seem that the culture of the academy—in Weiner's day and our own—makes it difficult to present novel and creative works in one's early research, and that it compounds this difficulty by treating graduate students as employees first, and scholars second.

Ventures such as the Society of Fellows are called for today, given the diffusion of distance-learning models, the capital-intensive quantification of 'output' and teaching performance, the erosion of the Arts and Sciences model for the sake of lucrative institutes, the outsourcing of teaching jobs, and the earmarking of research by corporate sponsors. The tendency is to reify education by reducing possible choices and roads of academic diversity. An unfortunate corollary to this is a trivialization of L2; at many colleges and universities today there is a rapid increase of short-duration study abroad programs; while ever more students are studying abroad, far too few of them are prepared in the languages of the host countries.

The Art of Categorial Thought

One's goal in learning a language is the mastery of skills which, once assimilated, are phased out of active conceptual thought. Mauro Ceruti writes in this regard of the complementary views of a system provided by internal and external observers:

The point of view inside the system is the point of view of the autonomy, organizational closure, maintenance, and reproduction of its own identity. The disturbances are not instructive inputs, but simple priming indices integrated into the organizational dynamics of the system according to the reproduction of this same organization. The point of view of an observer external to the system is the point of view from which the problem of the integration of the system in a metasystem is posed, the point of view of the transformations and evolution of the system. (Ceruti, 1994, p. 102)

Ceruti actually provides a good working definition of the transdisciplinary, a kind of map of the boundary areas between disciplines.[10] Without forcing a sameness of the languages of the arts and sciences, I envision a mutual respect for the pattern that connects, a language of polity to reflect the human ecology of the university. This means adopting a categorial thought that is constructive, though its various sublanguages— of philosophy, chemistry, linguistics, etc.—are fragmentary. As Ceruti writes,

Categorial thought, understood as constructive thought which gives form to the matrices of knowledge, finds its roots in [a] sort of principle of more general complementarity [...] in order to account for the relationships between the *results of knowledge* on the one hand and the explanation of their *epistemological condition* on the other. This principle can be found in the general mechanism whereby knowledge, in a stage of its acquired, organized development, perpetrates the greatest covering up of its true, genetic constitutive matrices. (Ceruti, 1994, pp. 74–75)

This fact of 'covering up' is critical to the argument I am proposing concerning probity, modesty and the recognition of gaps in learning.

The language and logic usually attributed to the exact sciences is atemporal and insufficient for understanding or adequately theorizing the realm of mind. In his discussion of the need for scientists to reinvigorate their interdisciplinary awareness of other fields, Stephen Toulmin suggests that the 'principle of non-contradiction,' which is a *formal* characteristic of some disciplinary methods, has been mistakenly construed to be a *substance*:

In the twentieth century, too, analytically-minded philosophers continued to prefer fields of experience in which our beliefs could be given a quasi-geometrical foundation to those in which that seemed imposssible. Once more, disciplines like Physics came out ahead, and were seen as intrinsically rational, while the rationality of fields such as Ethics, in which no agreed analytical proofs seemed to be available, was called in question. (Toulmin, 2001, p. 163)

To respect categorial thought is to continue in a tradition of humanistic research that assumes argument by ampliative inferences and novel hypotheses to be critical. It is to reaffirm that art is not simply desirable, but essential to teaching; that creative habits are intrinsic to a systems theory approach which considers the questions of emerging knowledge, deutero-learning and metacognition; and that philosophy is not an arch-discipline but is complementary to the other disciplines. In this way one avoids the error of confusing the vehicle that conveys information with the information itself. Such an error is all too common in the current age of theory, which has seen the emergence in the humanities of an impenetrable professional jargon. In the literary field, George Steiner offers the following critique:

> Those who proclaim and apply to poetic works a 'theory of criticism', a 'theoretical hermeneutic' are, today, the masters of the academy and the exemplars in the high gossip of arts and letters. Indeed, they have clarioned 'the triumph of the theoretical'. They are, in truth, either deceiving themselves or purloining from the immense prestige and confidence of science and technology an instrument ontologically inapplicable to their own material. They would enclose water in a sieve. (Steiner, 1989, p. 75)

Erudition (*episteme*) matters little if one lacks the practical ability (*phronesis*) to transmit its complexities. Confronted by the difficulties of learning a new language, students discover how to make their first language more expressive and coherent. As the guide in this process the language educator is obliged to follow the exigencies of art. As with any art, such a pedagogic practice is effective because it possesses its own intrinsic form. To truly exploit the performative and factual aspects of L2 in the classroom is to collaborate with students in a kind of adventure. As seen, the art of teaching 'language' across the disciplines requires a radical morality that is not always supported in today's university. To be the drum-beater or *paraiyan* (Tamil) is to risk being labeled a pariah. But there is much satisfaction to be had in the affective knowledge and empathy that one gains from teaching a language in such a way as to optimize the student's awareness of language as such, and thus by optimizing the student's abilities to learn how to learn. There is also, if one is lucky, a daily confirmation of Kenneth Burke's intuition that, '[T]he future is really disclosed *by finding out what people can sing about*' (1984, p. 335).

Notes

1. Cited in Cassirer, p. 148: '*Wer fremde Sprachen nicht kennt, weiß nichts von seiner eigenen.*'
2. See Whitehead, 1968a, p. 205: 'The function of art is to turn the abstract into the concrete and the concrete into the abstract. It elicits the abstract form from the concrete marble. Education, in every branch of study and in every lecture, is an art.'
3. See Hamrick, 1988, pp. 242–43: 'One new aim of education must then be to resist imitating the incomparably more interesting and vivid electronic media to distinguish what goes on in the classroom from time-compressed, disjointed, non-sequential presentations of subject matter. Rather than being entertainers for immediate pleasure, we need now to emphasize stability instead of novelty, order instead of change, and constancy in place of instancy.'
4. Ibid., p. 63. Similarly for A. N. Whitehead, 1968b, p. 1: 'Philosophy is the product of wonder. The effort after the general characterization of the world around us is the romance of human thought.'

5. Proctor cites the following books as models for his work: S. Toulmin, *The Return to Cosmology: Postmodern Science and the Theology of Nature*, Ernest Becker's *The Denial of Death*, Bateson's *Steps to an Ecology of Mind*, and the anthology *Habits of the Heart*, edited by R. N. Bellah.
6. See Whitehead, 1929, p. 58. 'In a sense, knowledge shrinks as wisdom grows: for details are swallowed up in principles.'
7. See Gardner, 1999, p. 113: 'It would be congenial [...] if the missions of schools could be stated clearly in terms of roles, values, notational skills, disciplinary knowledge, and an understanding of the true, the beautiful, and the good. However, we often fail to state what is intuitive or self-evident to us. Moreover, much of the most important curriculum is hidden—rarely spoken about, conveyed instead by the behaviors and attitudes of the older individuals in the environment.'
8. See Whitehead, 1968a, pp. 218–19: 'This discussion rejects the doctrine that students should first learn passively, and then, having learned, should apply knowledge. It is a psychological error. In the process of learning there should be present, in some sense or other, a subordinate activity of application. In fact, the applications are part of the knowledge. For the very meaning of the things known is wrapped up in their relationships beyond themselves. Thus unapplied knowledge is knowledge shorn of its meaning.'
9. See Dewey, 1944, p. 192: 'The notion that the "essentials" of elementary education are the three R's mechanically treated, is based upon ignorance of the essentials needed for realization of democratic ideals. Unconsciously it assumes that these ideals are unrealizable; it assumes that in the future, as in the past, getting a livelihood, "making a living", must signify for most men and women doing things which are not significant, freely chosen, and ennobling to those who do them; doing things which serve ends unrecognized by those engaged in them, carried on under the direction of others for the sake of pecuniary reward.'
10. See Ceruti, 1994, p. 102: 'If [...] the observer external to the system can formulate the problems of the transformation and evolution of the system, problems—which are rather insignificant from the point of view within the system—on the other hand it does this exactly on the basis of its ignorance of the detail of what occurs within the system from the point of view of the system itself.'

References

Barthes, R. (1989) *The Rustle of Language*, trans. Richard Howard (Berkeley, University of California Press).

Bateson, G. (1972) *Steps to an Ecology of Mind* (New York, Ballantine).

Bateson, G. & J. Ruesch (1951) *Communication. The Social Matrix of Psychiatry* (New York, W. W. Norton).

Bateson, M. C. (1994) *Peripheral Visions. Learning Along the Way* (New York, Harper Collins).

Becker, E. (1973) *The Denial of Death* (New York, Free Press).

Bellah, R. N., Madsen, R., Sullivan, W. M., Swidler, A. & Tipton, S. M. (1985) *Habits of the Heart: Individualism and Commitment in American Life* (Berkeley, University of California Press).

Brinton, C., ed. (1959) *The Society of Fellows* (Cambridge, MA, Harvard University Press).

Burke, K. (1984) *Attitudes Towards History* (Berkeley, University of California Press).

Cassirer, E. (1970) *An Essay on Man* (New York, Bantam).

Ceruti, M. (1994) *Constraints and Possibilities. The Evolution of Knowledge and Knowledge of Evolution*, trans. A. Montuori; Foreword by Heinz von Foerster (Lausanne, Switzerland: Gordon and Breach).

Dewey, J. (1944) *Democracy and Education* (New York, The Free Press).

Dewey, J. (1991 [1910]) *How We Think* (Amherst, NY, Prometheus Books).

Foerster, H. von (1984) *Observing Systems*, introd. by F. Varela (Seaside, CA, Intersystems Publications).

Gadamer, H-G. (2001) Education is Self-Education, *Journal of Philosophy of Education*, 35:4, pp. 529–38.

Gadamer, H-G. (1975) *Truth and Method*, trans. G. Barden and J. Cumming (London: Sheed & Ward).

Gardner, H. (1999) *The Disciplined Mind. What All Students Should Understand* (New York, Simon & Schuster).

Hamrick, W. S. (1988) Postliterate Humanity, *Process Studies*, 17:4, pp. 242–43.

Harries-Jones, P. (1995) *A Recursive Vision: Ecological Understanding and Gregory Bateson.* (Toronto: University of Toronto Press).

Kramsch, C. (1993) *Context and Culture in Language Teaching* (Oxford, Oxford University Press).

Margulis, L. (1998) *Symbiotic Planet: A New Look at Evolution* (New York: Basic Books).

Morin, E. (2001) *Seven Complex Lessons in Education for the Future* (Paris, UNESCO).

Nardone, G. & P. Watzlawick (1993) *The Art of Change Strategic Therapy and Hypnotherapy Without Trance* (San Francisco, Jossey-Bass).

Pert, C. B. (1997) *Molecules of Emotion*. Foreword by Deepak Chopra (New York, Scribner).

Proctor, R. (1998) *Defining the Humanities. How Rediscovering a Tradition can Improve our Schools. With a Curriculum for Today's Students* (Bloomington, Indiana University Press).

Scholes, R. (1998) *The Rise and Fall of English: Reconstructing English as a Discipline* (New Haven, Yale University Press).

Steiner, G. (1989) *Real Presences* (Chicago, University of Chicago Press).

Toulmin, S. (2001) *Return to Reason* (Cambridge, MA, Harvard University Press).

Vico, G. (1990) *On the Study Methods of Our Time*, trans. with introd. E. Gianturco; preface by D. P. Verene (Ithaca, NY, Cornell University Press).

Vico, G. (1993) *On Humanistic Education (Six Inaugural Orations, 1699–1707)*, trans. G. A. Pinton & A. W. Shippee; introd. by D. P. Verene (Ithaca, NY, Cornell University Press).

Walker, G. & M. Noda (2000) Remembering the Future: Compiling Knowledge of Another Culture, in: D. W. Birckbichler (ed.), *Reflecting on the Past to Shape the Future* (Lincolnwood, IL, National Textbook Company), pp. 187–212.

Weiner, N. (1950) *The Human Use of Human Beings* (New York, Doubleday).

Whitehead, A. N. (1925) *Science and the Modern World* (New York, Free Press).

Whitehead, A. N. (1929) *The Aims of Education and Other Essays* (New York, MacMillan).

Whitehead, A. N. (1958) *An Introduction to Mathematics* (New York, Oxford University Press).

Whitehead, A. N. (1968a) *Essays in Science and Philosophy* (New York, Greenwood Press).

Whitehead, A. N. (1968b) *Nature and Life* (New York, Greenwood Press).

7
Philosophy as Literature

JIM MARSHALL

Introduction

David Hume was both surprised and disappointed that his *A Treatise of Human Nature* 'fell dead-born from the press' without even exciting 'a murmur among the zealots' (Copleston, 1964, V(II), p. 64). The treaty was not received as a literary endeavour. Hume was disappointed because he did not draw a distinction between philosophy and literary works. But, even if that was a view held by some influential thinkers then, times have changed. The historical causes of these changes might be said, at least, to be the perceived priority in philosophy of epistemology post Kant, the rise of science, the accompanying emergence of philosophy of science, and the early work in logic of Frege, Russell and, arguably, the Wittgenstein of the *Tractatus*. These gave rise to what is now known as analytical philosophy, and which became a major aspect of the core in what can be called (traditional) Anglo-American philosophy. This analytic approach to philosophy has been mainly accepted within the (academic) English speaking world and came to almost dominate other approaches to philosophy in the middle and late 20th century. There are of course dissenters. On the other hand it did not penetrate deeply into European philosophy. Thus Bertrand Russell (1948, p. 819) said of 1929 French Nobel Prize winner, Henri Bergson, in his *History of Western Philosophy*, that he was irrational (Bergson was given an Honorary Doctorate from Cambridge in 1920 and Russell, himself, was also awarded the Nobel Prize for Literature in 1950). Yet Bergson was extremely influential upon French philosophy, e.g. upon Gabriel Marcel and (the early) Beauvoir, and upon the liberal humanists with the notion of the embodied self. More recently the proposal to offer Jacques Derrida an Honorary Doctorate at Cambridge was contested, amongst considerable uproar (see *The Times*, 9 May, 1992).

Most literary writing cannot meet the criteria of analytic philosophy, especially epistemological criteria. Yet many writers in the literary tradition present or work with philosophical ideas, and it is that literature which is our concern. Indeed it might be argued that a number of those writers within the literary tradition who have been recognised as 'great' writers have presented philosophical ideas; Shakespeare to Milton to ... Joyce, Lawrence and Orwell. This causes them, along with those philosophical dissenters in the English speaking world, to be categorised by the 'real' philosophers as at best second level philosophers, or perhaps for them to be cast outside the philosophical world altogether, as barbarians without the gates. Yet this has not been the case in European philosophy.

It should be noted that I am not talking about all literature, all literary works, drama, art etc. But I am talking about those literatures directed *primarily* at philosophical ideas, or the human condition, as opposed to literature addressed primarily to entertainment. I would not deny that the distinction on the widest literary spectrum between philosophical literature and literature in general is hard to draw.

But we can give examples at the ends of the literature spectrum. At the philosophical end of the spectrum, philosophy as literature as I will call it, we might place André Malraux (1933), Simone de Beauvoir (1990) and George Orwell (1949). At the other end of the spectrum we might place the musical, 'The Sound of Music', the play 'The Mouse Trap' and novels which either use philosophical ideas (Duffy [1987] uses Wittgenstein), or merely set a story in a philosophical setting, e.g. Marks (2001). I would call this end of the spectrum the entertainment end. Clearly the dividing line between the two sides of the spectrum is hazy, but perhaps no more than that between e.g. the colours blue and green. I believe that there are good clear examples of literature as philosophy (see below).

In what follows I will use the term 'literature', to cover *writing*, i.e. novels, essays, journalism, poetry and drama (including dramatic, film and TV productions) that express or depend primarily upon philosophical ideas. I have excluded art, music, opera, and dance from this paper, mainly because I am not clear as to how I wish to discuss these areas of the performing arts. What I am certain about however is that philosophical ideas can be and are presented in these art forms. As Sartre puts it in relation to art itself, in *What is Literature?*, if we are concerned with an 'effectiveness' in transmitting philosophical ideas, then:

> ... that masterpiece 'The Massacre of Guernica', does anyone think that it won over a single heart to the Spanish cause? And yet something is said that can never quite be heard and that would take an infinity of words to express. (Sartre, 1988, p. 28)

Sartre continues in the same source, in parallel vein, in the essay entitled 'For Whom Do We Write?': '... one writes for the universal reader, and we have seen, in effect, that the exigency of the writer is, as a rule, addressed to *all* men [sic.]' (Sartre, 1988, p. 71). But writing, particularly *academic* philosophical writing, is not addressed to *all* people. It is almost deliberately not so addressed. In the Introduction to *What is Literature?*, Steven Ungar comments as follows:

> '*What is Literature?*' addresses the question of audience—For Whom does One Write? ... To this end, Sartre sees that *littérature engagée* must adapt to the to the media and technology of mass communication ... there is a *literary* art of radio, film, editorial and reporting ... we must learn to speak in images, to transpose the ideas of our books into these new languages ... if not, he or she can expect to be read only by the bourgeoisie. (Ungar in Sartre, 1988, p. 15)

Sartre, Beauvoir and Camus, amongst others, met these criteria (note *engagé* carries a stronger moral or political sense than the English term 'engaged'). Education is a practice or institution which is clearly *engagé* and philosophy of education, which is normally seen as a normative enterprise within education, is even more *engagé*.

How then, if we accept Sartre's almost prophetic suggestion, are we as philosophers of education to approach literature *as* philosophy? Two questions at least can be raised at this point that might be discussed in the relationship between philosophy and literature? These are 'opening' questions—one is philosophical and the other is educational—and are not meant to be exhaustive of the possible questions. At best in rejecting some approaches, in the spirit of Sartre, and looking at approaches that might fit his criteria we can lay out a more catholic philosophical framework for further enquiry. These questions are respectively:

1) how does analytic philosophy approach literary writing?
2) how might philosophical ideas be presented in literature?

To answer these questions I will turn first to an analytic philosophical approach to James Joyce's 'Araby' (from the *Dubliners*). Second I will look at the way in which philosophical ideas are presented in French literature, and by Albert Camus and Samuel Beckett in particular. Finally I will discuss the lost opportunities in merely approaching *Dubliners* with a set of analytic assumptions.

1. An Analytic Approach to Literature

I will use Lowell Kleiman's and Stephen Lewis' (1992) book, *Philosophy: An introduction through literature*, and as an example of my concerns, discuss their treatment of James Joyce's 'Araby'.

In the preface to their book they say (1992, xiii):

> We have attempted in this book to offer beginning students the best of philosophy through the medium of literature. The two disciplines are natural allies—philosophy supplying perennial themes raised anew from one generation to the next, literature providing vivid illustrations of the meaning and poignancy of abstract thought ... we introduce each part with one or two literary selections that raise the philosophical issue. Second, in order to make the alliance work, we have been careful to pick the right combination of literary piece and philosophical scrutiny.

If the disciplines are meant to be 'natural allies' it is clear that one ally is in a subservient position. Yet both Sartre and Beauvoir were adamant that literature was superior to philosophy (Beauvoir, 1948, pp. 153–4). The literary selections in this book however are meant to illustrate certain things about philosophical ideas, and apparently not to present them, or consider them as possible new candidates for the analytic canon. Second they are meant to raise the philosophical issues for later abstract, and perhaps mathematical, analysis. Each part has a literary introduction, a literary extract, a series of questions about the literary extract, a philosophical discussion about the issues raised in the literary extract, further extracts, discussion questions and suggestions for further reading. This seems to represent an excellent framework. In my view Part 3, 'Personal Identity', is a good exemplar of this structure.

There are 62 extracts in this book of which 8 might be interpreted as *literary* (in my sense) and the remaining are extracts from philosophical texts. Aren't they also literary? Well that is one of the problems with this book. There is an assumed cleft between philosophical texts and (other) literature and they are at best said to be allies. Their use of literary texts is not so much to see what the author thinks *philosophically* and what philosophical ideas the text assumes or uses but to use the text for traditional philosophical analysis. I will illustrate this by reference to 'Araby', which appears in Part I of the text, entitled 'Knowledge'.

'Araby' is the story of a young man who is infatuated with the elder sister of a friend, Mangan (the text provided accords with the text in *Dubliners*). The young man is the narrator of the story. Whilst there are descriptions of the girl's physical attributes—'her dress swung as she moved her body' (p. 6)—the descriptions of their 'relationship' are all those of the young man; his manœuvres to see her and observe her, and of his own mental states which describe his infatuation. There is no indication initially that she has any interest in the narrator. However the sister eventually speaks to him and asks if he is going to the Araby market. It is clear that she wants to go but can't because she has to attend a retreat. Finally the boy says that he will bring her something, though she does not ask for anything.

One of the good things about Kleiman and Lewis' book is the guidance given to the assumed philosophically unsophisticated reader by the authors, and the questions for discussion also provided by the authors, whether one agrees with them or not. The first question on this section, and the first in the book is (p. 9):

> What *objective* evidence is there in the story concerning Mangan's sister's attitude towards the narrator? (Kleiman & Lewis, 1999, author's emphasis)

My first comment would be on the use of 'objective'. Why 'objective', and why the emphasis on that notion? Given that it is the first question and that there are many philosophical extracts to follow on the nature of knowledge in Part I, is this ordering a preparation for a certain view of knowledge? Is the knowledge that the boy has of his own inner states and feelings of no account? Is this self-knowledge not objective?

The authors' introduction to this literary account puts this possibility down. They say that he is a young boy moving into adolescence and becoming aware of his own sexuality. But it is not *said* in the text that he is an adolescent. The authors say that the sister is *somewhat* older than the brother. But it is only said in the text that she is an elder sister. Nor is it said in the text that the brother is the same age as the narrator—only that they play together. It is not even clear that they are in the same class or even go to the same school. What is clear is that the narrator goes to school alone. Thus Mangan might have been one or two years younger and the sister the *same* age as the narrator. He may be becoming aware of his sexuality but the account of his inner states might well pertain also to besotted adult males.

They also claim that the narrator's final comment namely 'I saw myself as a creature driven and derided by vanity' (p. 9), shows that he has been a fool in his belief that Mangan's sister could be seriously interested in him (p. 5). The reason given depends upon a pointless conversation between a female stallholder and two young men at the market, which the narrator overhears. But another conclusion can be drawn from the text of 'Araby' (see below).

What we have here is an analytic treatment of a beautiful piece of writing. (Unfortunately the authors' summary of the text is not very good as there are several things said by them that are not in the Joyce text.) All that seems to be sought from the reader are answers to traditional philosophical questions about knowledge, belief and evidence. There are no questions concerning the philosophical issues presented by Joyce in 'Araby'. Are they of no concern? Has this piece of literature been included merely to provide a text from an important writer for analytic critique? I will return to this issue in section 3.

2. Philosophy and Literature in France

The French do not make a fundamental distinction between philosophy and literature. John Cruikshank (1962) notes that between 1935 and 1960 in French literature there was an attempt to respond coherently to breakdowns in traditional beliefs, including morality and long periods of political unrest. There was France's demoralising defeat in WW II, and the subsequent political uncertainties of occupation and resistance, the Cold War, Europeanization, and the rebuilding of France. There was the accelerating pace of scientific developments, the invasion of common sense by the social or human sciences, the death of God, and the invasion of business and government by economic theory and theories of management. The literary response was not merely nihilistic though it was seen in that way by readers who were disoriented by what might be called the new writing of fiction. But the point here is that these authors are concerned with a number of lived human concerns, and their approaches to these concerns. These were not the approaches of Anglo-American philosophers.

Following Cruikshank I will mention a group of French writers who raised a series of important philosophical issues in their works on these issues, including the relationships between literature and philosophy. That troubled area where, in French writing, literature and philosophy appear to meet, was occupied by a number of French writers. Cruikshank identifies Georges Barnonus and André Malraux as the precursors of this 'occupation', and as successors or 'occupiers' Raymond Queneau, Jean-Paul Sartre, Samuel Beckett, Maurice Blanchot, Simone de Beauvoir, Jean Cayrol, Albert Camus and Alain Robbe-Grillet. Cruikshank's choice is not absolute or exclusive as others might have been included in his text, though he seemed to exclude André Gide and François Mauriac (Cruickshank, 1962, p. 3). Only three of these might be said to be philosophers who met the Anglo-American canon of being a philosopher—Beauvoir, Camus and Sartre— though often that accolade is granted grudgingly. For example, neither Beauvoir nor Maurice Merleau-Ponty is mentioned in Walter Kaufmann's *Existentialism from Dostoevsky to Sartre* (1956), though Albert Camus is mentioned (but Camus often denied that he was a philosopher). In Paul Edwards' comprehensive philosophical encyclopaedia, *The Encyclopaedia of Philosophy* (1967), the only mention of Beauvoir is a reference to her *Ethics of Ambiguity* (1948), which is said to be not only important in its own right but also in relation to Jean Paul Sartre (arguably *Pyrrhus and Cinéas* [1944] is more important). There is no further amplification or discussion in that source of what is said to be an important work and how it was related to Sartre—a crucial philosophical issue, because Fullbrook & Fullbrook (1994) challenge the standard account that Beauvoir was subordinate to Sartre and argue that she was an independent thinker—for example arguing against his notion of absolute freedom (see, her memoirs and *The Second Sex*: see also Simons, 2004).

So this troubled philosophical area is not the prerogative of philosophers *per se*, even French philosophers. But from the Anglo-American tradition the philosophers were outweighed even further because only Sartre, and grudgingly, would seem to qualify within the Anglo-American tradition (Kaufmann, 1956: Edwards, 1967). I exclude Camus *here* because of his own protestations that he was not a philosopher. Furthermore it is hardly likely that these writers had occupied this space for the reason of merely questioning the relationship between literature and philosophy. The interpretation of these works was that they were nihilistic.

Even those writers whose responses to these areas of concern were not nihilistic were usually interpreted in that way. There is a problem of course over what nihilism is, as to its meaning. But, on the assumption that we can understand it and progress for now, this response may have arisen for at least two reasons. First because these writers often describe a social world that many readers do not and cannot share— the world of Beckett's tramps in *Waiting for Godot*, or of Sartre's prisoners in *No Exit* [*Huis Clos*], for example. Second, they are often describing an alien form of human experience and what it means to be a human being against that form of experience—for example, Meursault in Camus' *L'Étranger*. Given that the form of these experiences is often quite disturbing and alienating, it is hardly surprising that the account of human beings is almost incomprehensible. Finally, the assumed nature of literature to entertain, to evoke pleasure, and arguably to reassure, is gone.

Albert Camus claimed that he was not a philosopher. He was a journalist (especially as editor of the resistance newspaper *Combat* from 1942), essayist, novelist, playwright and in *The Myth of Sisyphus* (1942) and *The Rebel* (1951) at least, philosopher. Furthermore, as Sartre said of Camus in his obituary he was: 'the present heir of that long line of moralists [which] perhaps constitute what is original in French letters' (Sartre, 1965, p. 109f.).

I use Camus here because he was a distinguished playwright. If we refer to his drama *Caligula* (1962), we can identify a number of philosophical ideas with which the reader or audience is presented, including the exercise of unbridled power. In Camus' drama, Caligula, the young and handsome Emperor of Rome, has had his faith in a benign universe shattered. His reaction to this *absurdity* of life is not to lie down in nihilistic fashion as if absurdity is an *end*, but to revolt. But it is not the revolt against absurdity that Camus advocates. Instead Caligula abandons the demands of traditional logic, morality, and humanity and with unlimited and unbridled power at his disposal he embarks on an indiscriminate campaign of cruelty, torture and murder. Thereby the philosophical attack upon unbridled or absolute power is brilliantly advanced on the stage, through drama. This is not just an illustration of a philosophical issue, because the drama itself encompasses and advances the argument.

It can of course be argued philosophically but the point here is that of *effectiveness*, of the grasping and understanding of a philosophical problem and of a philosophical position. Anyone who has seen *Caligula* on stage would surely come away with the equivalent of an effective philosophical argument on absolute power.

Samuel Beckett has a different answer to the absurdity of life from (Camus') Caligula. The notion of the theatre of the absurd is of course attributed to Camus, but for Camus the realisation of the absurdity of life was not an end point but *rather* a starting point. If absurdity was the starting point for Caligula, it was not Caligula's direction of revolt that was taken by either Camus or Beckett. This is quite clear in Beckett's *Waiting for Godot*. (See also the two approaches to nihilism which Camus contrasts in his 'Letters to a German Friend' [1962].)

The absurd in Beckett's drama is the situation of the two tramps, Estragon and Vladimir, waiting for Godot. They have few resources, little intelligence, medical problems, and no knowledge either of who Godot is or when he (or she) might be coming. Their position falls into the notion of the absurd. But in Beckett's drama this does not mean that nothing can be done. They must organise and order their lives in spite of this absurdity as the waiting (absurdity) is not an end in itself but a beginning, no matter how bleak their future might be. This is the philosophical message that I take from Beckett.

3. Literature as Philosophy

In this final section I wish to return to my original questions, which were:

1) how does analytic philosophy approach literary writing?
2) how might philosophical ideas be presented in literature?

The first philosophical question has been dealt with in section 1 but more will be said here. The second educational question will be raised by my reading of how Joyce presents philosophical ideas in 'Araby' and how the presentation of a human situation 'sites' the philosophical ideas in a recognisable context. This is a quite different reading of the Joyce abstract from that of Kleiman and Lewis. I have already commented on the 'errors' in their summary. I say errors because some of their points or claims are not explicitly said in the text, and are interpretations. But a different interpretation can be given to 'Araby'.

'Araby'

Kleiman and Lewis treat 'Araby' as a question of muddled beliefs for none of which the narrator has evidence, yet clearly believes that he knows them to be the case. The remaining seven questions for discussion (p. 9) are also about knowledge, beliefs and evidence. But that is a very limited reading of 'Araby'. Of course analytic analysis can be applied to literary texts. But if the assumptions underlying that analysis are those of traditional Anglo-American philosophy—as is clear in the selection of extracts in this book—then perhaps Kleiman and Lewis' analysis (p. 5) and their questions (p. 9) are what naturally follow. Let us look at a different reading of 'Araby'.

When Mangan's sister asks the narrator if he is going to the market, says that she can't go because of a retreat, and that 'its well for you' (p. 7) she may have been making an approach to talk to him about something which they might have done together. It could have been a shared interest and outing. So she is urging him to go. The narrator misreads the situation and thinks that if he brings her something she may talk with him and pay him some attention. But she did not ask him to do any such thing. However she has already broken a barrier between them, not by mere talk, but by raising the possibility of shared interests and outings. It can be argued that she wanted to enter into some form of human relationship with the narrator. It is because of the pointless banter between the people at the market stall however that he realises that he had not appreciated her approach to him and possibly that his offer to bring her something destroyed the possibility of any such relationship. That is why his 'eyes burned with anguish and anger'.

If you start with a non-analytic approach to philosophy, e.g. the Socratic notion that philosophy is mainly concerned with the self and the care and improvement of the self, with personal identity and its relationship with the Other, then you might come out with something like this reading of 'Araby'.

The analytic analysis does not attempt to identify Joyce's philosophical ideas in 'Araby', whereas the second does. It does not merely analyse the text for answers to questions about objectivity say, but presents several issues about the human condition. First we have a narcissistic young man, possibly a boy, or possibly an adolescent (but a creature driven by vanity [p. 9]). The narrator takes every opportunity to observe Mangan's sister—in modern parlance we might say he was stalking her. He believes or imposes upon her an identity in which she is really interested in him. That is part of his narcissism—her relationship to him is needed by him.

Second, at the market stall he realises from the pointless banter what has gone wrong with himself and Mangan's sister. His vanity, his narcissism, had resulted in a self that could only see others as useful for his own purposes. Initially this is how he interprets their discussion, but the market banter makes him realise not only that she was communicating with him in offering to share interests and activities but also without the Other that his self was an impoverished self.

We should also site this story in early 20th century Dublin. She is a young Catholic girl with considerable constraints upon her. She has to attend the retreat for example. She may well have been interested in the narrator who, ironically, would then have been correct about her. That she approaches him may have been an attempt to stop an 'idiotic' situation of silent stalking. We are not told that but it is possible. Another reason may have been her younger brother who is said to tease her when called for tea. His teasing about a boyfriend may have been difficult for her and for family relationships.

So Joyce is talking about the importance of the Other in establishing personal identity, in caring for the self and in establishing good human relationships. But he is also talking about the ambiguity of these human matters and how they are not fixed in concrete. He is also talking of the difficulty of human relationships when one is growing up.

For those interested in how philosophy and literary writing might be better reconciled, Kleiman's and Lewis' book is not helpful. In its treatment of literary works it makes the standard Anglo-American philosophical moves, asking questions about 'Araby', which, based upon traditional Anglo-American assumptions about knowledge and logic will surely lead in a chosen direction, and Joyce's 'Araby' is reduced to a set of mistaken beliefs. But that detracts from 'Araby''s richness and the ambiguity of Joyce's writing that, in turn, reflects the ambiguity and ever-changing nature of human relationships.

Of course the tradition is concerned with personal identity—Hume wrote on it after all—but the person and personal experience is not the starting point for most Anglo-American philosophy. Yet that approach has been in philosophy since at least the time of Socrates.

Conclusion

It should be clear that I do not see the 'natural allies' position of Kleiman and Lewis as providing any solution to the rift between philosophy and literary works. The natural allies position not only perpetuates this rift but places literary works in a subservient position (Rather like the positioning of 'inferior' colonial troops in times of war.). Both Sartre and Beauvoir believed that literature was superior to philosophy, though for different reasons (Beauvoir, 1948). Kleiman and Lewis see philosophy and literature as allies (see quote above) but relegate literature to the status of mere *illustrator* of abstract philosophical thought. I have tried to show through another analysis of 'Araby' that this is condescending and unsatisfactory. It is condescending because it ignores the philosophical worth of Joyce's writing. Similarly it would be rather pointless to analyse Camus' *Caligula* in such a manner. Camus does not provide explicit arguments against unbridled power—instead he pursues it in ways that provide a counter 'argument' to such practices and behaviour. His 'argument' is not an illustration of an abstract philosophical idea but *presents* directly, and in a different form from traditional philosophy, the ideas of nihilism and unbridled power.

The educational question has been posed but not answered. It has been presented as an issue of how to present philosophical ideas to people, especially the young. It would be tempting to reduce that issue to one of teaching and learning, and for some educationalists this might be reduced to testing the effectiveness of understanding engendered by seeing Camus' *Caligula*, say, and reading some philosophical essays on power. But what is important is not just knowing that unbridled power has nasty consequences but of affecting an *attitude* towards it and its effects. That is a notoriously difficult aspect of the curriculum. We introduce the young to novels, poetry and drama but the outcomes for some people are the purchases of *The Racing Times*, the reciting of doggerel limericks, and 'participation' in TV reality shows.

The teaching of philosophy has, in the main, been through the teaching of the history of philosophy. In epistemology, for example, one moved through the idealist, realists, and empiricists to the more modern problem solving approach (with variations from Russell to the later Wittgenstein and Ryle). The live shows were the visiting professors, symposia, and seminars, and the occasional TV interviews with important thinkers. Questions of meaning, justification and valid arguments dominated. But that is not everyone's cup of tea. Nor is the question of how to teach philosophy merely a philosophical question—to be decided by philosophers.

If philosophy is concerned with how one is to lead one's life then its teaching must recognize that there is more than questions of meaning, justification and valid argument that need to be 'transferred' to the young. For human beings, embedded in the fabric of discourse in a natural language, there are such things as beliefs, prejudices, aversions, desires, emotions, states of minds, intentions and motives, vagueness, ambiguity, rhetorical and polemical approaches and body language. Literature *and* Philosophy jointly can present ways of life that may be successful in navigating such uncharted waters (see e.g. the writings of Simone de Beauvoir, especially her early stories on young people, in Beauvoir, 1982).

References

Beauvoir, S. de (1948) *The Ethics of Ambiguity*, trans. B. Frechtman (New York, Philosophical Library). Originally published as *Pour une morale de l'ambiguïté* (Paris, Gallimard, 1947).

Beauvoir, S. de (1989) *The Second Sex*, trans. and ed. by H. M. Parshley with introduction by D. Bair (New York, Vintage). Originally published in two volumes as *Le deuxieme sexe* (Paris, Gallimard, 1949).

Beauvoir, S. de (1982) *When Things of the Spirit Come First* (New York, Knopf). Originally published as *Quand prime le spirituel* (Paris, Plon, 1979).

Beauvoir, S. de (2004) *Pyrrhus and Cinéas*, in: M. Simons (ed.), *Simone de Beauvoir, Philosophical Writings*, pp. 77–149. (Originally published Paris, Gallimard, 1944).

Beckett, S. (1954) *Waiting for Godot* (New York, Grove Press).

Camus, A. (1962) *Caligula* (New York, Knopf). Originally published as *Le Malentendu, suivi de Caligula* (Paris, Gallimard, 1944).

Camus, A. (1953) *The Rebel*, trans. Anthony Bower (London, Hamish Hamilton). Originally published as *L'Homme révolté* (Paris, Gallimard, 1951).

Camus, A. (1982) *The Stranger*, trans. K. Griffith (Washington, DC, University Press of America). Originally published as *L'Étranger* (Paris, Gallimard, 1942). An English translation gives the title as *The Outsider*. [This is a bad translation of the title in my view].

Camus, A. (1955) *The Myth of Sisyphus*, trans. Justin O'Brien, New York, Random House. Originally published as *Le mythe de Sisyphe* (Paris, Gallimard, 1942).

Camus, A. (1960) Letters to a German Friend, trans. Justin O'Brien, in *Resistance, Rebellion, and Death* (New York, Alfred Knopf). Originally Published as *Lettres á un Allemand* (Paris, Gallimard, 1948).

Copleston, F. (1964) *A History of Philosophy*, Vol. V, Pt. II (London, Burns & Oates).

Cruikshank, J. (1962) *The Novelist as Philosophe: Studies in French fiction 1935–62* (London, Oxford University Press).

Duffy, B. (1987) *The World As I Found It* (New York, Tickner & Fields).

Edwards, P. (1967) *The Encyclopedia of Philosophy* (New York, MacMillan).

Fullbrook, K. & Fullbrook, E. (1994) *Simone de Beauvoir and Jean-Paul Sartre: The remaking of a twentieth century legend* (New York, Basic Books).

Hume, D. (1898) *A Treatise of Human Nature*, ed. L. A. Selby Bigge (Oxford, Clarendon Press).

Joyce, J. (1987) *Dubliners* (Harmondsworth, Penguin).

Kaufmann, W. (1956) *Existentialism from Doestoevsky to Sartre* (Cleveland & New York, Meridian Books).

Kleiman, L. & Lewis, S. (1992) *Philosophy: An introduction through literature* (St. Paul, MN, Paragon House).

Malraux, A. (1933/1961) *Man's Fate* (New York, Random House). Originally published as *La Condition Humaine* (Paris, Gallimard, 1933).

Marks, T. (2001) *Theoretically Dead* (Norwich, VT, New Victoria).

Orwell, G. (1954) *Nineteen Eighty Four* (Harmondsworth, Penguin). (Originally published London, Secker & Warburg, 1949).

Russell, B. (1948) *A History of Western Philosophy* (London, George Allen and Unwin).

Sartre, J-P. (1965) Albert Camus, trans. B. Eisler, in: *Situations* (London, Hamish Hamilton).

Sartre, J-P. (1988) *What is Literature?* (Cambridge, MA, Harvard University Press). Originally published in 6 instalments in *Les Temps Modernes*, 17–22, 1947.

Sartre, J-P. (1989) *No Exit [Huis Clos]* (New York, Vintage).

Simons, M. A. (2004) (ed.) *Simone de Beauvoir: Philosophical writings* (Champaign-Urbana & Chicago, University of Illinois Press).

Index